LOVELY STA

"MY QUEST FOR THE TRUTH"

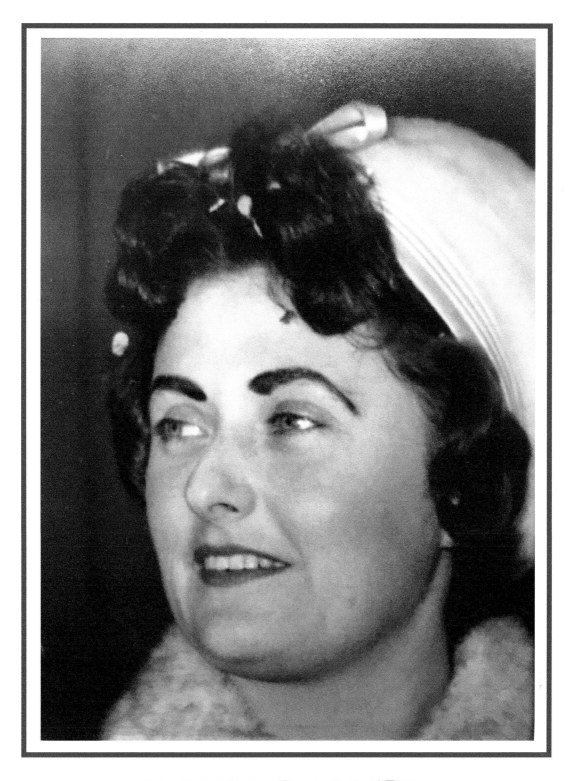

JOHN BARKER

PUBLISHING INFORMATION

John Barker has asserted his right under the Copyright, Designs and Patent Act 1988
to be identified as the author of this work.

Copyright © John Barker 2022

British Library Cataloguing In Publication Data
A catalogue record for this book is available from the British Library: ISBN 978-1-7396046-1-5

Published by:
P3 Publications
13 Beaver Road
Carlisle
CA2 7PS

Printed by:
Book Printing UK
Remus House
Coltsfoot Drive
Woodston
Peterborough
PE2 9B

A book for my lovely Stanella

My

LOVELY

STANELLA

...given
away
as a baby

...and denied a home in a Scottish mansion with an Irish fortune to go with it...

LOVE AND HAPPINESS CAME IN AN ENGLISH COUNCIL HOUSE

Anne Clenaghan could be proud of her striking beauty – her Irish beauty - and proud too of passing on that beauty to Stanella, her baby. Sadly, that beauty was all that she did pass on. The luxury life Anne enjoyed in the Clenaghan family mansion she denied to Stanella. And she denied a mother`s love. To her eternal regret, Anne gave Stanella away.

Stanella, left with only her mother`s striking beauty was alone now - her father was nowhere to be seen. She grew up to become no ordinary girl. Within the Henderson family which took her in and brought her up, she stood out as someone who was very different.

Stanella was as different from the Henderson family as that family`s three bedroom council house was different from Anne`s Scottish family mansion with its 120 rooms, where Mary Queen of Scots and a king of Norway both stayed.

The council house family had no royal connections. But the family gave a royal welcome to an abandoned baby. And they kept on giving. They denied nothing. Stanella got wealth to last her a lifetime and much more. It was the precious wealth of love.

HELLO DARLING

Today, many years later, I lean over Stanella as she lies nearly asleep. Her eyes open and she smiles. To my surprise, she says: "Hello darling". She hasn`t spoken much for the past month because a terrible illness has caused havoc in her brain. I reply:"Hello darling". I stroke her cheek and think that there is little left of Stanella, the lovely wife I loved. The lovely wife I loved has been reduced to little more than a skeleton with her brain almost blocked out by six horrible years of dementia.

In the first of those six years she was tormented by anxiety and depression. She thought the answer was the drug, Valium. She had previously taken Valium and found it calming and soothing to her troubled mind. But not this time. Several prescriptions of the drug later, the anxiety and depression, far from disappearing actually got worse. Doctors refused any more Valium.

Two days later there was another transformation. The anxious and depressed Stanella became very aggressive, almost an animal. Every member of the family was attacked continuously like a tornado. Terrible rows in the family followed. Household knives were hidden and outside doors locked. We were warned by a doctor to call the police if the aggressive behaviour got out of hand.

A memory test for Stanella was arranged by doctors but she failed dismally. A doctor prescribed other drugs to calm her down. But it was all to no avail. Eventually the police were called to stop Stanella attacking anyone in the house. A policeman stayed for most of a day and his presence had a calming effect.

Doctors tried to find her a place in a local mental health unit but no place was available.

Stanella`s attacks continued and our son Jonathan decided to sleep at our house to prevent any of Stanella`s night attacks. Almost every day, a GP was requested but doctors who attended were confused. They could not decide whether the behaviour was the result of a mental condition or the first symptoms of some form of dementia? It was hard to tell.

A brain scan was arranged after about eight weeks of unruly behaviour. Finally Alzheimers was confirmed. To some extent that was a relief because doctors then could prescribe drugs aimed at relieving the illness.

But there was no cure.

A HOME THAT VANISHED

During her illness Stanella insisted many times on "going home," That was not the home she had lived in for the past forty years. Nor was it to her two previous homes. No, the home that Stanella insisted on returning to was a home that vanished about half a century earlier when her parents died. It was the home of her childhood, a three bedroom council house.

Several times every day during her illness she started to move towards the outside door. I asked her where

Stanella`s most loved home- 11 Ridgemount Road, Carlisle, a post-war council house.

she was going. She replied: "I am going home". "But this is your home" I would say. "You have lived here for forty years". "No, this is not my home" she would reply emphatically and make another dive for the door.

I pushed her back and, as always, she would tell me that her home was in fact with her mother and father in the house where she lived as a girl and young woman before she married and where she always said she spent her happiest days.

That home vanished half a century earlier. But it had been a very well-loved home. Stanella, given away as a baby nearly ninety years ago was lovingly brought up in that home by Bessie Henderson and her railwayman husband, Jimmy. They took her in, gave her love in abundance and gave her a surname. But Bessie and Jimmy never managed to adopt her and may never had any thoughts of adopting her.

Bessie became Stanella`s "mother"and Jimmy became her "father." The couple died more than half a century ago and now every other member of that family is also dead.

Up to six years ago, Stanella knew she was the last of the Hendersons. But then her illness wiped that from her brain. She became overwhelmed by Alzheimers, living a cheated and deprived life, a life she had no hope of overcoming. But she continued to grope in her mind for ways to go back to the happy and secure years she had with Bessie and Jimmy. She thought she could simply walk back to that life and to that home.

Alzheimers had done the cheating and depriving. But long before that cruel illness, there had been cheating and depriving of another kind, some of it equally as cruel.

As I cared for Stanella and faced up to her latest attempts to leave our house and go back "home" I wondered about the many years of cheating and depriving her of any information about her real mother. Why had she had to wait until she was nearly 30 years old before she learned about her biological mother, Anne Clenaghan and that her name was not Henderson but Clenaghan?.

I wished I knew more about those early years of her life and the people who did the cheating and depriving.Most of all why did they do it?And then I was brought back to reality and I wondered about the next meal I had to prepare for her or the next medicine she was due to take.

People told me that looking after Stanella was far too much for me. If I go under they said, there will be no one to care for her and she will be put in a care home. But I was driven on by the thought that with me around, she was happy. With her medication, I made sure that she never knew pain. And I knew that all that I did for her was no burden to me.

Far from a burden, I was extraordinarily blessed .Stanella was as helpless as a baby to love completely and to care for completely. Some people have no one to love and care for and they become much smaller because of it. I say to her: "Do you love me?" "Yes" she replies. "But how much?" I ask. She says "A big lot."

I laugh and Stanella laughs.

BROUGHT HOME IN BASKET

The thoughts of a baby to care for sparks a memory of Babe, the name Stanella was always given by her father, Jimmy. I say: "Who was it who always called you Babe?" There is no reply and I answer for her: "It was your dad, Jimmy. Babe was the name he gave you when he brought you home in a basket."

Soon Stanella`s brain will be completely blocked out. She will be unable to speak and even possibly to think. What then will go on in her head I have no idea, just as I have no idea of her thoughts these past six years. I think that if her brain is blank and she has no thoughts she will be happy. She may then know that at last she has made the final exit from a tormenting time.

I stroke her greying hair, slowly making its way into her near - jet - black hair and catch a look in her eyes, now grey and dimmed from the stunning violet they were years ago. I comfort her with words I have used a thousand times: "I love you. I'll look after you and take care of you." She makes no sound but gives me another smile.

It`s a very precious smile which I treasure greatly for I fear that there will be not many more smiles. Smiles, like the few words she utters are fast disappearing, crushed by the cruel illness that offers no hope of recovery but a slow and certain decline to death. I back off a little and glance at at Stanella`s shrunken body. I again think that she looks just like a baby to be cared for.

Day after day I wash her, dress her, cook for her, feed her and sometimes battle with her to give her medicine. I do her hair, do her make-up, do her shopping, and keep tempting chocolate drops and green grapes heaped up in a dish at the side of her. I turn night into day for her because Stanella never can sleep at night. I chat to her at two in the morning and am chatting again at four and at six. I am always there for her.

And then there are the falls she is always prone to. I try always to be alert and on hand to block and prevent them. Sometimes I fail and things turn nasty. Things turned very nasty with her fall over a Christmas tree and the broken femur it caused. That fracture put her in hospital for a fornight. But there were many others.

The worst fall of all was when she got ouside the house at three in the morning and ended up lying in the gutter with a smashed face and a smashed arm and five weeks in hospital. She came near to being trapped in her ward with no visitors allowed because of the terrible Covid pandemic that hit the nation and the rest of the the world in February 2020.

Because of the pandemic, serious restrictions on movement were imposed on much of the country, particularly on hospitals where often no visitors were allowed.

JOURNEY OF DISCOVERY The story of that journey home in a basket nearly a century ago stuck with Stanella. The journey was so extraordinary that it was remembered for many years by her friends and family. It was a journey that shaped her life for ever. For me as Stanella`s husband that journey also marked the start of another journey. That journey was to find out why Stanella ended up in that basket in the first place after being given away as a baby when she was six months old.

Perhaps the basket side of the story is not strictly true because a six month old baby would need something much bigger than your average shopping basket. But the story was widely circulated as true by members of Bessie`s family.

Stanella herself, before her fatal illness - we suspect it started about eight years ago - was as curious as me about that basket journey. But whenever it was mentioned, she held back from trying to find out more about it. She would go quiet, or change the subject. She feared what she might discover. And she also feared that she might fatally disturb some relationship she knew nothing about.

 My journey of discovery about Stanella`s Scottish Clenangan family background lasted two years. It involved many letters, emails, phone calls and long discussions with people who knew Stanella. And it also involved discussions with members of her mother`s Irish family, which was another branch of the Scottish Clenaghan family.

The family came from from the city of Lisburn near Belfast more than a century ago, and because they were Catholics they suffered greatly from the arson attacks and other troubles in the early years of the twentieth century. One branch of the family – Stanella`s branch - escaped the troubles by settling in Scotland, first in Ayrshire and then in nearby Dumfriesshire.Another branch of the family escaped the troubles by moving to Dublin.

The Clenaghan family today is big and widely scattered. All of those members I have contacted have been very helpful and very kind in coming forward with information about their fathers, mothers, brothers, and sisters.

This kindness in many ways is surprising in view of the fact that nearly all of these family members knew nothing of Stanella`s actual existence. Stanella`s existence had been kept a secret to most of the family members, but not to all.Surprisingly, the first that many of the family heard of Stanella`s existence was a phone call or an email from me soon after her death on October 12 2020. She was 87.

From that unexpected contact many of the family learned to their amazement that they had a completely new female relative who had been hidden away from them for more than three quarters of a century.

Happily, there has been much more to my search than finding undiscovered relatives. There has been my discovery of a historic eighteenth century Scottish mansion, Terregles House, situated in the historic border village of Terregles near Dumfries where most likely Stanella would have been brought up had she not been given away.

TERREGLES...`PLACE OF THE CHURCH`

The name Terregles means "place of the church" and comes from the ancient Welsh language spoken in the Nithsdale area of Scotland during the Dark Ages.

Terregles House had 365 windows, 120 rooms which included 14 bedrooms, four servants` rooms, and its own laundry and chapel. It was the home of the Scottish Clenaghan family. This consisted of Stanella`s mother Anne, Anne`s parents and her ten other brothers and sisters.

Before the blast! Terregles House as the Maxwells knew it.

Swan Lake- garden water feature of Terregles House in the background.

Takeaways are off - dining in style with the aristocratic Maxwells at Terregles House.

Left: Once blooming, now derelict-Terregles House gardens during the Maxwell dynasty.

Below: Fountain feature of Terregles House garden in the Maxwell era.

There was no mansion for Stanella. As I wrote earlier, she spent her childhood and the years up to her marriage in a three bedroom council house on a Carlisle estate built in the years immediately after the Second World War.That council house was no different from hundreds of others on the same estate. Terregles House on the other hand stood alone as a large, historic and very impressive stately home.

That house and two previous houses on the same site had been occupied for several centuries by a Scottish aristocratic family, the Maxwells. It was their family seat.

There can be few greater contrasts than a council house and an historic Scottish mansion. But more than a mansion, Terregles House had something else. It had a colourful history in its own right as a historic home. It had a close connection with a famous queen, and a king and many other notable people over the centuries.

A member of the Maxwell family, Lady Winifred Maxwell became very famous in 1715 after she rescued her husband from the Tower of London where he had been held as a condemned prisoner. I have dealt with the rescue in more detail later in the book. And in 1746 Lady Winifred became famous for a second time when she rescued Bonnie Prince Charlie after the battle of Culloden.

The famous queen was Mary Queen of Scots who in the 1560`s twice visited a castle, which was one of the earlier Terregles Houses on the same site. After the second visit, the queen left for England for help, but instead was executed. When the Scottish poet Robert Burns lived in nearby Dumfries, he was a frequent visitor to Terregles House.And he wrote a song about it.

The king was King Haakon VII of Norway who lived in Terregles House during World War Two with many of his troops. At the time his country had been overcome and occupied by the invading German army.

Soon after the war, the Maxwell family abandoned the mansion when, it is thought, they could no longer afford to live there. Terregles House was taken over by Stanella`s mother`s family, the Clenaghans. From the Clenaghan relatives I have learned a great deal, particularly the family`s origins a century or so ago in troubled Northern Ireland.

Those troubles were responsible for Stanella`s grandfather James Clenaghan leaving his home in Lisburn and coming to live in the safety of Scotland where his big family was born and bred. Those troubles were also responsible for Stanella`s uncle, James`s brother, Hugh, leaving his home in Lisburn and going to live in the safety of Dublin.

The two brothers and the two families were kept together by a big and very successful cattle dealing business they ran for about half a century in three countries: Northern Ireland, the Republic of Ireland and Scotland.Cattle dealing, an historic home and family and the sometimes horrific troubles in Northern Ireland are all bound up in the story of Stanella, an Irish girl who was conceived in Scotland and given away as a baby to eventually become an English girl.

All the things that I have learned about the life of Stanella and her biological family I have tried to put together in the pages of this book .I hope that you find the story interesting.

A PRIVATE NURSING HOME

Baby on the way-Stanella`s birthplace,12 Chiswick Street Carlisle, once a maternity home.

First, let us go back to the journey of the baby in the basket....

Leading up to that journey, according to Stanella's family, there had been emotional scenes in Nurse Catherine Clarkson's Nursing Home, 12 Chiswick Street, Carlisle, an Edwardian five bedroom terrace house where Stanella had lived for the previous six months. She was born there on November 29 1932.

Private nursing homes such as Mrs Clarkson's, which was also known as a maternity home, were fairly common in the years before 1948, the year the National Health Service came into being in Britain. Many private nursing homes were run by doctors. Some expectant mothers of course, could not afford a maternity home, particularly if they were unmarried. Some of the unmarried in the Carlisle area ,however, managed to get a place at a Church of England maternity home, St. Monica's at Kendal, 52 miles away.

Others went to Coledale Hall in Newtown Road, Carlisle which was run by Carlisle Diocese Council for Social and Moral Welfare. At Coledale Hall, girls were trained for domestic service or, if homeless, were found a refuge and given help. The Coledale Hall annual report for 1932 - the year Stanella was born - said that 100 girls and ten children were helped during that year.

Nine of them, some of school age, were returned to their relatives, eight were sent to a maternity home, five were sent to other homes or institutions, and 15 entered domestic service. Nine babies were sent to fathers or mothers of the new mothers and 38 outside girls were helped with affiliation orders. Girls from outside the home paid 710 visits to the home.

The report gives an example of the help given to one girl who was deserted by her boyfriend after the two had become engaged. After the birth of her baby, the girl was placed in service and a foster mother found. "For three years the child has been entirely supported by the mother, who is now happily married and the child lives with her and her former boyfriend, now her husband," says the report.

But many of these illegitimate birth stories were completely different. "Alone and ashamed" was how one similar unmarried mother of that era described her plight many years later in a reader's letter to The Times newspaper in June 2021.

A state of "moral disorder" is how the same situation was described in 1932 in the Coledale Hall report. The report has this to say: "Our social worker knows that many cases of immoral practice are never brought to light. This state of things leads us to think that the education of thinking people, as responsible people in regard to moral questions, is one of the great needs of our time as responsible people seem to be largely unaware of this new symptom of moral disorder.

ONE OF ELEVEN CHILDREN

Stanella's mother, Anne, was 22 when she gave birth, living in Terregles House, 36 miles away from Carlisle. When Stanella was born the house had been sold by the Maxwells ten years earlier to Anne's father, James as I said a highly successful and wealthy Irish cattle dealer.

Anne, sadly, had been unable to plan properly for the baby because she was a single mother and life for single mothers in those days was not easy. It was particularly not easy for Anne because her father, James, was not only an influential businessman but a leading Roman Catholic and life at home was very

Stanella's grandparents, James and Annie Clenaghan, pictured in 1921.

12

Front row, left to right: Patricia, Dorothy, Bridget and Freddie.
Middle row, left to right: Mary, John, Norah, Margaret, Anne and James.
Backrow, left to right: James Clenaghan and his wife, Annie + baby Sheila.

strict, according to other members of the family. James would almost certainly have done something about it had he known that Anne was pregnant, according to Anne`s elder sister Margaret, in conversations she had with Stanella half a century later.

There was also the gossip among friends and neighbours to be taken into account. How Anne felt as an unmarried mother is probably best explained in that letter to the Times which I mentioned earlier.The letter says this: "She [the mother] was made to feel by society that she had shamed herself and her famiy by having sexual relations outside marriage.

"She had been incompetent and thoughtless, why else was she pregnant? Her lover had deserted her so she must be worthless to him and indeed, who would marry her after this illegitimate birth? Additionally, because she often had to hide from family and friends she was alone in her decision making. Self-worth was low, the future bleak.

"Society, including the child`s parents, teachers and future friends would consider the child as less for being illegitimate and the mother an embarrassment. Forcing was not necessary to achieve agreement to adoption.It seemed the only good thing to do for one`s baby. The paper work and the signing away of one`s child was hell. All that remains 50 years on is deep grief" says the letter.

In Anne`s case, adoption was not much discussed as far as I can find out. But her plight was outlined many years later by her Aunt Sheila, now more than 100 years of age, the only surviving member of James Clenaghan`s family. Sheila told her daughter Moira that Anne was the most beautiful girl in the family and always well turned out. "She was also very kind and nice," said Sheila.

So it sounds as if it must have broken her heart to have given up Stanella.

The Coledale Hall 1932 report, mentioned earlier, is strongly against adoption. It has this to say: "In connection with our work among unmarried mothers, we should like to point out that we do not encourage the adoption of illegitimate children as we believe that no work is truly remedial which relieves a girl from the responsibilities of motherhood."

A very hard attitude, many people would say today.

"RAILROADED" INTO ADOPTION

Anne`s plight as a single mother has very recently been highlighted along with the plight of an estimated 250,000 other women in Britain who were coerced into giving away their babies in the years just prior to the Second World War and the years immediately after that war.

One of these women was a former Labour MP, Ann Keen. At the age of 17, she became pregnant by a married salesman. Her horrified parents sent her away to give birth, forcing her to hand over her child for adoption. She was told she had brought shame upon her family in her small village in Flintshire. She was sent to the other end of the country to a church - run centre for unmarried pregnant women.

While there, heavily pregnant, she was forcd to scrub steps and scolded every day by the staff who reminded her that she was selfish and bad. Now she wants an apology for herself and for thousands of others who suffered the same fate.

The Parliamentary Joint Committeeon on Human Rights announced in July 2022 that it has examined the issue of forced adoption and it has agreed that the government should apologise to unmarried mothers 'railroaded' into adoptions.The Joint Committee said it acknowledges the "grave wrong" done to mothers and their children who "still live with the legacy of suffering".

An estimated 185,000 children were taken away from unmarried mothers and adopted between 1949 and 1976 in England and Wales. The joint committee added that the Government "bears ultimate responsibility for the pain and suffering caused by public institutions and state employees that railroaded mothers into unwanted adoptions".

The mothers had to endure a cruel double dose of shame. First, the shame of getting pregnant out of wedlock and second, when society's attitude to unmarried mothers changed, they were judged for supposedly not caring about their babies and giving away their baby.

Joint committee chairwoman and Labour MP, Harriet Harman, said the bond between mothers and babies was "brutally ruptured" over the three decades, and the adoptions "should not have happened". She said: "The mothers' only 'crime' was to have become pregnant while unmarried. Their 'sentence' was a lifetime of secrecy and pain.

"They were told they had 'given' their baby for adoption when they had done no such thing. Their child grew up being told that their mother had 'given them away.' Ms Harman said the committee acknowledges the "grave wrong" done to mothers and their children, adding: "It is time for the Government to do the same and issue the apology they seek".

Right: Stanella`s mother Anne- aged about 22 and a new mother.

ANNE`S SECRET LIFE

Stanella, as I said earlier, was never adopted and it is not known whether any pressure was brought against her mother, Anne, to get her adopted. From what I have learned, her pregnancy can be traced to a "secret life" she had been living, according to her younger sister, Margaret. That "secret life" came from her love of dancing and her regular attendance at afternoon dances in nearby Dumfries.

Margaret told Stanella: "Anne was crazy about dancing. She used to get me to go along with her to Dumfries, pretending we were going to the city library. I cannot recall why the dancing had to be kept secret. Whatever the reason, we went to Dumfries with our books every week with Anne`s dancing shoes hidden among them.

"As I had no interest in dancing, I went to the library with the books and Anne went to the dance at the Plaza in High Street, now the site of the former Debenhams. We met up again afterwards." Margaret thought that it was at one of those dances that Anne met the man who was to make her pregnant with Stanella. Margaret said she had no idea who that man was.

That may have been true, but equally may not have been true because the two sisters were very close and undoubtedly shared secrets. Margaret told Stanella: "I don`t think the family ever found out who he was. At home he was generally referred to as `The Rotter.`"

Anne`s "secrecy" continued during her pregnancy. She had her meals, not with her family but with the servants. And when the baby was due she chose to have it, not in Scotland but 34 miles from home, in Carlisle, over the border in England. Or, possibly, according to Margaret, that decision was made for her by her mother, Annie, herself once a single parent called Annie Tonner before her marriage to James Clenaghan.

Or that decision may have been made for her by her father.It was common at that time for the parents of un-married pregnant daughters to send the girls many miles from home where the birth could be arranged, as happened in the case described earlier of the former Labour MP, Ann Keen.

After the birth Anne was told by her mother Annie, that she needed to get the situation resolved. She knew from her own experience as a single parent of the difficulties that lay ahead for Anne and the baby, who by then was called Stanella.Anne never explained how she came to choose that name. Stanella, of course, is a combination of her own name, Anne and Stella.

Searches on the internet found no other Stanellas. But there are thousands of people called Stella, the name by which Stanella eventually came to be known.

Anne, I feel sure, never brought her new baby back to Terregles House. She was faced with the absence of support at home so had no choice but to leave the baby at the nursing home or stay at the nursing home with her. Which course was taken is not known but, according to Stanella many years later, six months were to elapse before a decision was made about where Stanella was to go.

Staff at Nurse Clarkson`s nursing home who had helped to look after Stanella since she was born came up with ideas.Naturally, adoption is likely to have been considered because six years previously it had become legal for the first time. Many adoptions before then, and also afterwards, were arranged informally by organisations or through individuals such as doctors, nurses, lawyers and the local vicar, or they were arranged between the birth mother and the adopting parents.

However, in the case of baby Stanella, one of the nursing home staff, Sarah Beattie who was a cleaner at the home, came up with what turned out to be a perfect solution. Sarah said she knew of a woman who she thought was very suitable for taking the baby and bringing it up. She was Sarah`s niece, Elizabeth Jane Henderson, generally known as Bessie, a Carlisle mother who had just lost a baby girl through still-birth and was prepared to give Stanella a home.

COMPETITION TO HAVE STANELLA

There was still one hurdle to overcome. It was a surprising and unexpected hurdle: there was competition within Bessie`s family to take Stanella and give her a home. Nelly Gill, a sister in law of Bessie, let the family know that she also was prepared to give Stanella a home.

From discussions in the family many years afterwards it seems the competition between Bessie and her sister in law was quite keen, particularly as Nelly was unable to have children and was desperate to start a family. And Stanella by all accounts was a very pretty baby. Why Bessie won the "competition" and became Stanella`s "mother" is not known. But the loss of face by Nelly and her resentment at failing to take the baby rankled with her for a long time, according to Stanella who spoke of it many years afterwards.

Stanella said then that Nelly had always been an embarrassment to her. "Nelly constantly tried to live her life as close to me as possible, taking what to me was an unusually great interest in my home life and my education as I was growing up".

This great interest puzzled and confused Stanella who felt that somehow she"owed" Nelly something because of that interest. It was only many years later, after Stanella found out that Jimmy and Bessie were not her parents, that Stanella learned the reason for that unusually great interest .

Nelly told Stanella that she, just as much as Jimmy and Bessie, had also had wanted to bring her up and become her "mother." Nelly painted a glowing picture of how much better Stanella`s life would have been if she had been brought up in her home and not that of Jimmy and Bessie.

That glowing picture would have probably been true as far as material things were concerned because Nelly`s husband had an executive job on the railways-"a boss`s job" was how Stanella described it. That boss`s job gave him a status far above that of railway locomotive fireman Jimmy Henderson who finally became Stanella`s "dad."

Nelly and her husband frequently holidayed in the South of France and let it be known that she possessed genuine Chippendale furniture which was valuable.The Hendersons on the other hand had holidays at home, making do with a few days a few miles from Carlisle at nearby Silloth. And their furniture had probably been bought second hand.

Later in life, when Stanella first heard of the "competition" to bring her up, she told other members of the family that she was appalled to think that she might have ended up as Nelly`s"daughter." Stanella had no time for Nelly because of her niggardly, miserly ways. Stanella was anything but niggardly and miserly.

She was overwhelmingly generous with everything she had and was fiercely loyal to Jimmy and Bessie. She said: "I loved my mam and dad. I could not have been happy with anyone else."

So it was decided after long-drawn out family discussions that, after the Carlisle nursing home, Stanella should go and live with Bessie and her husband Jimmy, a London Midland and Scottish railway loco fireman, soon to be promoted to driver. Arrangements were made and, according to the family, Jimmy, a handsome six footer in his forties came to the nursing home with a basket and carried Stanella away.

He called her Babe as he chatted to her on the way. And he continued to call her Babe to the end of his life.

A MOVE TO BLACKPOOL

Jimmy`s journey with his newly-acquired Babe took about ten minutes and when he arrived at his two up and two down railway terrace house home, 82 Brook Street, there was much anticipation and excitement about the new member of the family.

Jimmy and Bessie had been married for just a few years. Bessie, a widow, had two sons, George and Brian Smith from her previous marriage to John Sydney Smith, a barman. She had lost a baby daughter a few months earlier.

A family move to Blackpool, 100 miles away from Carlisle, came shortly afterwards. It was caused by Jimmy`s work, although some members of the family believed that Jimmy had asked for the move so the family could in some way "hide" Stanella. They feared that Stanella`s mother would try to take her back. And they thought that Blackpool was less accessible than Carlisle.

It was at Blackpool that a letter arrived from Anne, posted from Terregles on May 17 1933, six months after Stanella`s birth. It is the only surviving letter from Anne and was addressed to Bessie. It said that Anne had been on holiday in Dublin where an aunt and uncle lived with their family.

This is what the letter says: "Dear Mrs Henderson. Many thanks for your letter and postcard. I would have written sooner but I came on here after returning from Dublin. I had indeed a wonderful time and hope to go back soon again. Tonight I go back to Annan so my address will be as usual.

"So glad you like your new house- you certainly get plenty of changes! Mother thinks I ought to get Stanella adopted as I will never have any chance of ever taking her myself. Dear Mrs Henderson, can you give me any advice on the matter. I really don`t know what to do and for her own sake I do want her to have a mother and a father and a name.

"How are you all keeping? Well, I hope. Enclosed please find £3. Give Stanellas huge kisses from me. I would dearly love to see her again, but it is better if I don`t. Write soon Mrs Henderson and give me all news. Good luck and best wishes.Yours sincerely, Anne."

Below and opposite: a photocopy of the only surviving letter from Anne.

It was about the time of this letter that Bessie became pregnant again. And Bessie soon found she had two babies to care for. The new baby was called Roy. He had Stanella`s pram and baby clothes waiting for him when he arrived and he and Stanella grew up together sharing the pram and baby clothes, and of course everything else.

Despite the thoughts expressed by Anne in the letter, the Hendersons had a constant fear that Anne, would return and take Stanella back. It made for a lot of uncertainty at Blackpool for Jimmy and Bessie.

CONSTERNATION AS ANNE ARRIVES

There was in fact a "threatening" move a few years later in another letter from Anne and her mother. They said they planned to visit the Henderson's Blackpool home in Norfolk Road and would be arriving by car. The letter caused consternation in the Henderson household. The planned visit posed a real possibity that they would lose Stanella.

Jimmy and Bessie had known for very long time that they had no "hold" on her. It is thought they had not gone ahead with adoption, possibly because they were unsure of how Anne would react, despite the views in the letter, if the subject of adoption was approached.

They may or may not have guessed correctly that Anne would not allow it - Anne and her mother had previously indicated that they might one day take Stanella back to Scotland. Back to Scotland was what Jimmy and Bessie dreaded. Stanella was by then a much-loved member of their growing family. In addition she had a new name given by the family.

That name came after the family realised that the name Stanella was proving difficult - a bit too much of a mouthful for them to manage. So instead, she was given a family name of "Sten," a name she kept to the day she died. Her father Jimmy however continued to call her Babe. People outside the family generally referred to her as Stella, which was the name she preferred.

As far as the dreaded visit by Stanella`s mother Anne, Jimmy and Bessie felt that their only hope of keeping Stanella would be if she could be encouraged to refuse to be taken away. And that exactly is what they planned to happen when Anne and her mother actually arrived.

Big girl now! Stanella the toddler

Many years later, Stanella recalled the visit and how aged about three, she refused to be taken away. She said: "Mam and dad told me several times that two smart ladies were coming in a big car to visit us. I was told to be very nice to the ladies but if they wanted me to go away with them I should say that I wanted to stay with mum and dad (Jimmy and Bessie) who of course were the only mum and dad I knew.

"Being so young, I had no idea then that the two smart ladies were my mother Anne and her mother. It was only many years later that I learned from Mam what actually had been going on. I certainly didn`t want to be taken away because I was so happy with my mam and dad. So, when the two ladies arrived, I did my best to hide behind mam`s dress. I stayed there while all the talking was going on. Of course, I had no idea what they were talking about."

Today, many years later, it is impossible to say how the conversation went, except to say that Stanella stayed put. Anne and her mother returned home to Terregles without Stanella.

But for Jimmy and Bessie it had been a worrying episode… a close-run thing. And it wasn`t to be the last worrying episode.

"MISSING" CHURCH COLLECTION

An episode that was far from worrying- very funny in fact- came from the closeness of the relationship of Stanella and her younger brother, Roy as they grew up together. Stanella always claimed that she took care of Roy. He in return was always able to help out with a loan or a gift of money when Stanella hit hard times.

To illustrate their closeness, Stanella often told the story of the missing church collection money and the "illicit" ice cream. The two siblings were about eight, and as usual on a Sunday morning they were on the way to church. Stanella had an idea. She said to Roy: "Let`s not go to church today. Let`s have ice creams instead."

How to pay for the ice cream was no problem - they would use the church collection money. So ice creams were bought and consumed. But neither of the two miscreants reckoned on the guilty look they both displayed on arriving home. Their father, Jimmy, was quick to spot this look. He asked the two of them if they had actually been to church and if they had, which priest had said the mass. He persisted with the question.

This was too much for Roy and he began to break down. Stanella remained silent. Jimmy again persisted, telling them of the seriousness of the situation and that if they did not tell the truth he was going to take them to the priest and get a confession that way. Fortunately the situation was quickly resolved. But the story continued to remain standard repertoire for Stanella, particularly when she was in the company of other people and Roy was present.

Roy on hearing the story re-told for about the fiftieth time would always laugh and blame Stanella. "All your fault" he would say."The ice cream was your idea. You led me off the straight and narrow".

GEORGE AND HIS BOSSY WAYS

The Henderson family`s stay in Blackpool lasted just a few years. But it was long enough for George, Bessie`s eldest boy, to win a grammar school place and then to have to turn it down because the family could not afford the school uniform and the books. George, born in 1923 at 94 Charles Street Carlisle, was not to be deterred. He was a a quiet boy, very intelligent, serious and industrious and he went on to do flying duties as a radio operator in the RAF during the Second World War.

**Stanella`s father**, Jimmy (right) with his wife, Bessie, and Bessie`s son George, and wife Georgie.

He served in the RAF for four years and returned to civilian life in 1946 to live with his family at Carlisle, first at 82 Brook Street, and later at 11 Ridgemount Road. He married in 1948, qualified as an accountant and ended his career as chief accountant of the British office of the German chemicals giant, BASF.

George was always remembered by Stanella for the gifts he brought her as a girl from the various countries he served in while in the RAF. But he was also remembered for Peter, a budgerigar which he gave to Stanella and which she kept for many years.George was also remembered for keeping Stanella`s behaviour up to scratch, at least up to the high standards he set for her. He was nine years older than Stanella so it was not difficult to give her orders. Whether she obeyed those orders was another matter!

When the two met up many years later, Stanella was never backward in teasing George about his bossy ways particularly when he caught her eating fish and chips in the street. Not only did he try to correct her but he also reported to their mother that "Stanella had a deplorable habit...eating in the street!"

George might just as well have turned the other way and ignored Stanella and her fish and chips because she was defiant about such discipline. She might have accepted such discipline from her mother, but not from George, particularly as eating in the street, now of course as common as eating at home, was at that time starting to become an acceptable everyday activity.

Brian, George`s brother, was the opposite of George. He was a smiling, happy go lucky and very popular boy and a great friend of Stanella who was three years` younger. Brian served an apprenticeship with the Metal Box company as a toolmaker, did his national service in the RAF and later worked on the Blue Streak rocket project at Spadeadam, near Carlisle. He finally became became tool room manager with a company at Bingley (West Yorkshire) where he lived after his marriage.

Brian was so devoted to his Carlisle family that after he was married he would frequently leave his home in Bingley, drive 100 miles to Carlisle and then spend the day decorating his parents` house. Then he would drive back to Yorkshire and do a night shift at the factory where he worked.

His daughter Davida said of him: "His achievements should be measured not by what he did in his life but by how he lived. He was one of life`s enthusiasts. Always busy gathering friends wherever he went, he was club man and an outdoor boy."

Roy, Stanella`s third brother and a year younger never married but after his father`s death, continued to live with his mother in Ridgemount Road until her death. He then moved to a flat in a nearby street. Roy`s working life was spent with Edmund Fox, a Carlisle firm of motor factors. He did three years army service - from 1953 to1955 with the Royal Electrical and Mechanical Engineers, serving in England and Germany and rising to the rank of corporal.

His discharge certificate described him as "A Class 'A' Storemen with an excellent knowledge of technical stores. He is intelligent, sober, honest and trustworthy and can be thoroughly relied upon. He is a keen sportsman, smart in appearance and well recommended to any future employer."

LIFE IN "HAPPY VALLEY"

Bessie`s homesickness caused the Henderson family to leave Blackpool and return to Carlisle. Stanella was about six. Bessie missed her very supportive close family in Carlisle. So Jimmy got a job-move back to Carlisle and shortly afterwards the family moved into a newly- built council home, 11 Ridgemount Road, part of a cul-de-sac of about ten houses in Petteril Bank, a post-war city council housing estate.

It was here that Stanella spent some of her happiest years - not surpisingly, because the cul-de-sac was called "Happy Valley" by the families who lived there. These were the days of great civic pride on council estates. Many of the the people had up to very recently been wartime servicemen who had returned to civilian life expecting to be living in slum or inferior houses.

Now re-housed in homes fit for heroes, they were rightly proud of the excellent houses provided by their local council. Many of the families were badly off by today`s standards but what they did possess in material things they shared with each other, just as they shared their joys and shared their sorrows.

Sadly, many of the estates later became neglected and came to be known as sink estates, characterised by much crime and vandalism. Many estates were transformed yet again when the householders got the opportunity to buy their own homes.

Stanella`s happiness living at 11 Ridgemount Road was mostly derived from the love of her family. Her much-loved "mother" Bessie would almost daily send Stanella with a written note to one of the estate shops. The note would list food or other items the Henderson family needed. One the bottom of the note Bessie invariably wrote: "Something for Roy`s tea." Roy, of course, was Stanella`s brother.

The shopkeeper invariably would respond with another note and supply perhaps a meat pie or some cooked ham which he considered suitable for Roy`s tea. The shopkeeper invariably would also include in the order what he called "two fancies for Bessie." The "fancies" were fancy cakes given free by the shopkeeper who considered Bessie more a friend than a customer.

Stories like this invariably raise a laugh when re-told today. But they were part of the way of life in post-war Britain. Now, more than half a century later, it is very hard to imagine a Tesco store manager hunting for something for Roy`s tea!

Preparing teas for Roy and for other people kept Bessie very busy. It was for making teas that Bessie is best remembered by her relatives who regularly visited every week or so. On Mondays, her sister Kate was the regular visitor. On Tuesdays, very often it was her sister in law, Hilda. On Wednesday, it was her sister Doreen and on Thursday, sister in law Evelyn.

And so it went on week after week, visits that were a delight to Stanella, who was always a centre of attraction. The visits were lovingly remembered by her.

STANELLA WAS "SOMEONE SPECIAL"

Kathryn Gill, grandaughter of Bessie`s sister in law Hilda, also remembers the family visits. She told me: "I was just a little girl at the time but I well remember how my mother`s face always lit up whenever she talked about Bessie and her visits to Bessie`s home.

"I remember Stanella as being someone special because that was the way she behaved and the way she was treated. Everyone loved her and somehow knew of her special something, particularly because she was such a warm person and so outstandingly beautiful. "I think everyone in the family thought that Stanella was 'adopted` which of course she wasn't, as I have learned only recently. However, the subject was hardly ever discussed because everyone accepted her as one of the family.

"I vaguely remember some speculation about her birth family. One story which is in fact not true was that both her parents were students. I also remember one story that I feel sure was true... that Stanella as a baby was brought home by Jimmy in a basket from the nursing home where she was born.

Kathryn was very surprised about one thing: that Stanella had to wait for such a long time-she was in her twenties- before she learned that Bessie and Jimmy were not her parents. She told me: "I can however understand why that information was kept from her - she was not adopted and because of that, Bessie and Jimmy would have no official hold on her and they would be afraid of losing her."

Kathryn is a teaching assistant at St Margaret Mary`s Catholic Primary School in Currock, Carlisle. Through her job she has formed new links with Stanella who was, of course, her second cousin. The new links are two young girls who are sisters and pupils at the school, Imani Marshall aged 11, and Hunter Marshall aged 10. They are great grandchildren of Stanella- their father, Robin is the son of Stanella`s second son, Keith.

Both girls are pupils at St Margaret Mary`s and both bear a resemblance to Stanella. Kathryn describes Hunter as very graceful and says both of them are "rather special."

FOOTBALL IN THE STREETS

Just as the progamme of family visits to Bessie at 11 Ridgemount Road was repeated week after week, so also was the menu for the meals there. Invariably, afternoon tea comprised sliced tongue and salad, or possibly sliced ham and salad. This was always followed by tinned orange segments with Carnation Milk. Years later, Stanella, after she married me, continued Bessie`s afternoon hospitality tradition. She regularly invited Bessie, Kate, Hilda and Doreen to tea at our home, Lyncroft, in nearby Harraby Grove.

Back in Ridgemount Road, and two or three doors away from the Henderson`s number eleven lived George McVitie, slightly younger than Stanella, who was to achieve local fame. As a boy of about eight playing in the road outside his and Stanella`s homes, George was already showing football skills that eventually made him into a professional player.

George is now 74 and a retired postman. He has fond memories of life in Ridgemount Road and remembers Stanella and the others in the Henderson family, all of whom he knew and played with. He told me: "Looking back it seems that everyone living in that area was part of a big happy family, in and out of each others houses every day and sharing everything, even going on day trips with neighbours to Silloth.

"I was always playing football with my pals in the street. One of us would say say`coats down`and we would begin a game using our jackets as goalposts. My mam used to say that the only time I was in the house was to have a meal." That way of life has sadly vanished. And football on the street seems to have gone too. Obviously, with the amount of traffic it would be difficult, but there isn`t the same community spirit that we had half a century or so ago."

George and his soccer skills made him a neighbourhood idol. He won six England schoolboy caps and went on to play for Carlisle United, West Bromwich Albion, Oldham, and

GEORGE McVITIE CARLISLE

Queen of the South.This success wasn`t so unusual. Petteril Bank estate and neighbouring Harraby and Botcherby estates were rich in soccer talent.

Several youngsters, contemporaries of George, also became professional players, some of them playing for England. Possibly the most famous was the late Kevin Beattie of Botcherby who played for Ipswich and England and was, according to England Manager Sir Bobby Robson, the most talented player he ever handled.

Football was of no great interest to Stanella, unlike her father Jimmie and her brothers. They were all fans of the local professional team, Carlisle United. Stanella`s interests were more centred on her home. She attended St Cuthbert`s, a Carlisle Catholic primary school and went on to Margaret Sewell secondary school.

But happy schooldays to Stanella were not what most of us think of as happy schooldays. They were not the days she spent at school, but the days she managed to escape from going to school!

Stanella was a clever youngster. She was proud of the fact that she could read before starting school after teaching herself through reading the Daily Herald newspaper at home.And through all her schooldays she had no problems with learning, except that she did not like school. Why that was, she had no difficulty in explaining: "When they wanted me to go to school I always used to say `Why should I have to go to school when I am so happy at home with my mam?"

In most homes, that question would have been easily answered and then there would be no choice but to go to school. That applied also in the Henderson home to Stanella`s other three siblings who all excelled at school. Stanella was the exception and had a choice because she was strong-willed and defiant and also probably because of her background... a child given away, and still possibly without a a completely secure status in the loving Henderson family that had given her a home.

That family, particularly Bessie were always aware that they had no "hold" on Stanella because they had never managed to adopt her. And the fact that she might be "reclaimed" by her mother was an ever-present threatening cloud over the family. So Stanella became in effect a"spoiled" child, given far too much of her own way even in important daily decisions like schooling. The result was that she missed more school than most children.

Missing school resulted in Stanella losing out as the years went on and she under-achieved even after she left school. At the start that did not worry her but as she grew older and saw her less talented friends getting ahead of her, she came to realise that she lacked education through not going to school and regretted what had happened.

She used the days at home, not to be idle, but to give her mother, Bessie extra help around the house. Stanella always prided herself on her skills at housework and always got great pleasure in helping Bessie in any way she could. When she was no more than ten years old, she could "go through the house" as she put it and have the place as sparkling clean as her mother would have it.

Stanella had other skills. She was a very good dancer and could entertain herself for hours by dancing on her own in the kitchen. And from memory she could play any tune on the piano. She often regretted not having music lessons because the family could not afford them.

Another skill she had was that of a mimic. In the company of other people she never had any difficulty in getting a laugh by taking off someone well known. That was always accompanied by her continuous hand gestures. She became noted for these gestures and her far less demonstrative mother would jokingly comment: "There must have been a Frenchman somewhere in the family".

As an adult, Stanella excelled as a housewife and mother. But after her children had left home she had time on her hands and always gave the impression that there was something missing in her. What that something was she never said but she did make one or two attempts at taking up part time work. These came to nothing and seemed to leave her disappointed.

It was at her first school, St Cuthbert`s, that she met Shirley Pape who was about the same age and who who became her lifelong best friend. Their two homes were very close to each other, both of their families were Catholics, the two went through school together and each had babies on similar dates.

Stanella jokingly called Shirley "Pearly Shape." Their friendship lasted until Shirley`s death in 1993 and is remembered by Shirley`s family for the massive phone bills the family sometimes struggled to pay, all the result of interminable phone conversations between the two women.Shirley is also remembered by her gift to Stanella of a cut glass fruit dish and the loving final note with it she sent just before her death from cancer in 1992.

The note was dated: "Middle of the night."

It went on: "Fifty five years is a long time - though at the moment not long enough for me.However, friendship and love is what I have received from you over that time. I`m getting tired sitting out of bed with cold feet (don`t tell mother, she`ll be down with warmed socks and a cup of tea). Just to say `thank you Stella` All my love, Shirley." Shirley became a social worker after she had a family and Stanella often said she envied her. Stanella wished she had persevered more at school in order to get a a full-time job like her friend.

STANELLA`S MOTHER MARRIES

Times were not easy for Stanella`s family, particularly in the hungry nineteen thirties. The country was pulling out of the Great Depression and the city of Carlisle like most places had high levels of unemployment. But Carlisle was to some extent protected from the worst of the depression through being an important railway centre employing several thousand workers in that industry.

Railway jobs were comparatively secure and Stanella`s dad, Jimmy, continued in work as a London Midland and Scottish train fireman and on one occasion, fireman on the Royal Train. In connection with the Royal Train, Jimmy treasured the thank you letter dated October 28 1942, from the Chief Operating Officer of the London Midland and Scottish Railway Company, enclosing ten shillings "To mark the occasion of your working on an important private special train from Carlisle to Euston on 20th October 1942."

Jimmy eventually qualified as a driver.He was from Bury in Lancashire and through his work had moved to Carlisle where he met Bessie. One of his family was a professional footballer with Bury FC - he was known as Puzzle Henderson. Stanella as a girl spent holidays with her father`s family in Bury.

The outbreak of war in 1939 and the bombing that followed took its toll on Jimmy. Often he had to drive trains through the bombing. There were also incidents when he had to deal with army deserters hiding in the locomotive he was driving.

The outbreak of war also led to the wedding of Stanella`s mother, Anne in 1941. She was serving in the civil nursing reserve and married Noel Henry Nash, a RAF Volunteer Reserve aircraft designer from Weston - Super- Mare. The ceremony was on June 21 at the Church of St. Francis Xavier, Potters Bar, conducted by a Father Grande. "A large number of guests attended" according to the Dumfries Standard newspaper report of the wedding.

The report added: "The bride was charmingly dressed in a turquoise blue ensemble and, on leaving for the honeymoon which is being spent motoring in Devon and Cornwall, she wore a beige-coloured suit. The reception was held at Elstree Ways."

The couple had three sons. One was Gordon who died a few years ago. His widow Gillian lives in Ferndown, Dorset. Another son, Ian, a retired engineer is married to Pamela, a retired nurse. They have lived in Melbourne, Australia for 43 years and have two daughters, five grandchildren and three great grandchildren. A third son, Douglas, died in February 2020. He never married and lived with his parents in Hayling Island, Hampshire.

The sons never learned of Stanella`s existence until after her death in 2020 and then only Ian had survived. He was deeply shocked at the news. He told me in an email: "I am just recovering from the shock of a recent call I had from my sister in law, Gill, who informed me of the discussions she has had with yourself about the death of Stanella. "I am absolutely astounded that I have had a sister all my life who I have known absolutely nothing about whatsoever, so please excuse my ignorance. "I think the thing that I find disappointing is the fact that I had no idea about Stanella until now that she has gone. Up to recently my wife and I took regular trips to England to visit various family members. How sad that Stanella and I never had the opportunity to meet"

Ian asked me if I or any member of my family had ever attempted to contact their mother, Anne, while Stanella was alive. Sadly, the answer to that is no. The reason there had been no contact are quite simple. Stanella dearly loved the Henderson family which brought her up, particularly she loved her "mother" Bessie. She was always apprehensive that any probing of her past would harm that loving relationship.

She was apprehensive too of what shocks or surprises she might discover if she did that contacting. But most of all she considered the position of her mother Anne. She realised that it was very likely that Anne would have married after she was born. If that were so and she had not mentioned Stanella`s existence, news of her "secret" daughter would have been devastating for the husband and any possible children. She thought that the news could easily have ended the marriage.

Ian ends his email with an offer to help in tracing Stanella`s past. He said: "I hope that all I have said in this email will assist in piecing together a few more parts of the puzzle. "But please feel free to keep in contact, and I will be happy to assist in any way I can."

The Second World War years had brought marriage and a new life to Anne Clenaghan but to Anne`s daughter Stanella, the story of the war was mainly of schooldays. Her eldest brother George served in the RAF while elder brother Brian and younger brother Roy, like Stanella, spent the war years at school.

Brian was called up into the RAF near the end of the war to be followed by Roy who was called up into the army. For Stanella, one of the highlights of the war years was, as an eleven year old, winning a place to Margaret Sewell secondary school in Carlisle and the prize that went with it.

That prize became the subject of a story Stanella frequently told. It was the story of how Bessie, her hard-up mother managed to get the four pounds it cost to buy that prize. Bessie raised the money by scrubbing floors on her hands and knees in a bakehouse on Saturday mornings. Her efforts had been kept secret until the prize was actually purchased.

Stanella told the story of that purchase many years later. She said: "Mam decided to take me into the centre of Carlisle, saying we were going shopping. "But we did none of the usual shopping and she took me into Abbey Street, a street I hardly knew. "I was puzzled and asked Mam what it was all about. Mam didn`t answer but led me to T.P.Bell`s, the biggest bicycle shop in the town. It was then for the first time I knew that I was getting a bike. I was very excited".

The bike was an Elswick and from Stanella`s accounts later, no bike was more treasured than this one. She told of the many dustings and cleanings she gave the bike every day. She was particularly proud of her mother`s efforts. "My mam scrubbed bakehouse floors on her hands and knees to buy me a bike she would say proudly. Then she would add. "It was the best present I ever had from the best mam anyone ever had."

With the bike came a much more mobile Stanella...and her first boyfriends. The boys she met were aged about 11, her own age, all with new bikes and all keen to go on bike rides, very often to the local beauty spot, Wetheral, a few miles away, beside the River Eden.

However, Stanella was growing up into a very choosy girl. As a young teenager she didn`t always go for boys from near her home in Ridgemount Road. No, the boyfriends she chose were invariably from a bit further afield. From what Stanella said later, these boys had a bit more money to spend.

Not that Stanella could be called a golddigger. Up to that time she never had much money to spend because her parents never had much money and she was happy with that.

LOOKING LIKE MARGARET LOCKWOOD

But what Stanella did possess was outstanding good looks. As a teenager she was often said to look very like one of the 1940's leading British film stars, Margaret Lockwood. One noted similarity was Stanella's strong, long, dark and slightly wavy hair. That hair was her pride and joy and her proud boast was that she herself was able to keep it attractive - she never went to a hairdresser until her second marriage at the age of 28.

Possibly her single most attractive feature was her very striking violet eyes. People were struck by the beauty of those eyes seconds after meeting her. Those eyes, together with her very soft, very white skin and her strong dark wavy hair convinced Stanella that she had all the features of a typical Irish girl.

She had these thoughts years before she learned of her biological mother, Anne Clenaghan and Anne`s very Irish family. It was an instinctive feeling for the truth of her background long before she knew that truth. Stanella`s dress sense was immaculate. She dressed mostly in blue and white and more often than not in clothes handed down in the Henderson family or borrowed. Her legs invariably had to be painted - she couldn`t afford stockings.

A slight lisp added to the attractiveness of a stunning looking girl. But Stanella did not find her lisp attractive. She hated her lisp and a few years later, with a lot of determination and practice she managed to eliminate it.

Stanella`s mother Bessie always warned Stanella of the dangers that often followed for a girl who was pretty.

She said: "Mam told me that she was forever glad that she was not born pretty because she then had no problems of living her life with other girls – she could always be sure they were not jealous of her."

But there were still problems. Stanella was outstandingly pretty and had a lot of admirers. One who was a regular visitor to the Henderson`s Ridgemout Road home began to cause her embarrassment because of his attentions. "He always seemed to arrive at our home when I was arriving for lunch or arriving for my tea. I got thoroughly sick of him hanging around," she said years later."

"I tried several times to get him not to visit our house. Eventually I told him to b..... off."

The admirer was a handsome young Catholic priest.

Another admirer was Brian, a boyfriend of Stanella when she was about 12 years old - he was a businessman`s son from nearby London Road- and was always very keen to buy her ice creams and take her rowing on Hammond`s Pond, a few streets away from her home.

To her great surprise, Brian would suddenly have to leave her to attend a daily choir practice at Carlisle Cathedral. Stanella at that time never could understand the demands on a boy of daily cathedral choir practices which he had to attend.

However, a decade or so later she did eventually understand. Two of her sons, Bryan and Keith, were invited to join the same cathedral choir. Keith became the choir`s head boy.

Iain Clarkson, another young boyfriend and also a businessman`s son spent many meetings with Stanella teasing her about his Christian name. She was challenged by him to spell it, but she never could. Finally, Iain spelled it out for her and Stanella admitted she had never before heard of that spelling. He frequently took Stanella to the cinema but always insisted on the most expensive seats - seats that embarrassed her because she had never sat in them previously because she had never been able to afford them. Iain was related to Margaret Clarkson who ran the Carlisle nursing home where Stanella was born fifteen or so years earlier. Sadly, Iain had not long to live and died of cancer in his teens.

A third businessman`s son – Seamus O`Connell, who later became an England international amateur footballer - talked seriously to Stanella about marriage, although aged about 15 she had a couple more years to wait to go to the altar. So serious about marriage was he that Stanella was invited several times to his home to meet his mother. She was just as keen on a possible marriage as her son. But talk of marriage had no appeal to Stanella. She was as dismissive of Seamus as she was of the young Catholic priest who kept calling at her home. She told Seamus that he was really looking for another mother to care for him and she had no intention of assuming that role. Seamus was an Irish cattle dealer`s son. Stanella`s biological mother, Anne, as she was to learn many years later, was an Irish cattle dealer`s daughter.

Stanella`s most serious boyfriend before her marriage at the age of 17 was Tommy Little who was the same age as herself and like her came from a railway family. The Littles were friendly with Stanella`s family and lived in Charles Street just a short distance from Stanella`s home in Brook Street. Stanella and Tommy went around together for more than a year and were regularly together at a weekly youth club in the Elim Church in Edward Street near their homes. Elim Church youth club was preferred to other youth clubs in the area, according to Stanella, because its sandwiches tasted better than those at the other clubs.

In her later years, Stanella frequently spoke nostalgically of that club and others in the area and the complete lack of sophistication in the youth club activities she enjoyed. Stanella seldom drank alcohol and was disdainful of those who drank it to excess. She could never understand the need for alcohol by today`s teenagers and young women. "We were very happy with lemonade at the youth club- we didn`t need alcohol to be happy," she frequently said.

That apart, alcohol was not freely available to young people in Carlisle where laws about its sale were very strict. That strictness followed the nationalisation of all the pubs and other licensed premises in Carlisle and district. The nationalistion, by the wartime prime minister, David Lloyd George took place in 1916. Pubs became the property of the Home Office.

Controls over drinking were a matter of vital urgency for Lloyd George because drunkenness by munition workers from the nearby Gretna munitions factory was halting the suppy of shells to the army in France. The nationalisation continued until 1971 when the pubs were sold off by the Conservative government of Edward Heath.

Stanella`s father Jimmy, and Tommy`s father Hughie were work colleagues at Carlisle`s Upperby locomotive depot. Their job was to drive trains south from Carlisle, mainly to London, where drivers often had to stay overnight, and drive a train back to Carlisle the following day.

A sister and brother of Tommy, Mary and Hughie, became leading members of Carlisle Labour Party and for many years played a big part in the civic life of both the city and the county of Cumbria. Both were mayors of Carlisle and were the only brother and sister ever to become mayors of the city.

Hughie, who died a few years ago was also chairman of Cumbria County Council and was appointed an Officer of the British Empire (OBE) and a Commander of the Order of the British Empire (CBE) for his civic service. He was also awarded a medal from Carlisle`s German twin city of Flensburg.

Mary served as the agent of Ron Lewis who was the city`s MP from 1964-87. In 1983 he had the smallest majority in the country - a total of 63 votes ahead of his Conservative opponent.

Mr Lewis is remembered fondly for spending all his weekends in the city, combining his political life with his personal and religious life as a local preacher.

Each weekend he and his wife drove to Carlisle from their home 168 miles away at Langwith Junction in Derbyshire. Saturday was spent by the couple chatting to shoppers in Carlise city centre. Sunday was spent preaching at Methodist churches in the city.

It was in 1962, on one of Mr. Lewis`s visits to Carlisle - the day was November 29, Stanella`s fortieth birthday that he introduced Stanella`s youngest son, Jonathan, then aged three, to Harold Wilson, the then Prime Minister. It was a bizarre get together and is described later in the book.

Mary is now retired from public life and lives with her husband Jim Styth at Morton, Carlisle. She told me: "Stanella was two years older than me and I remember her as an outstandingly pretty girl. We played together as children and then got to know her better when she and my brother Tommy went out together. I have seen her several times since then and when we got together we chatted about old times."

Mary said that until a short time ago when she learned about Stanella`s birth family, she had no idea that Stanella was not a Henderson. "No one knew that. But had we known it would have made no difference because

Stanella was always a very happy girl with a happiness that showed that she was very loved by the family that brought her up."

Stanella`s first job when she left school at 15 was that of a telephonist in Binns, a Carlisle city-centre department store which later came part of the Frazer group. It was a job she loved. Later in life she mimicked herself and the slight lisp she had. "I would answer the phone calls saying `Binth of Carlisle.` And it wasn`t long before some of the other girls were calling me Binth of Carlisle" she said many years later.

MARRIAGE AT 17

When Stanella was 17 she decided to marry Keith Stuart Davidson (both left), a railway engine cleaner of about the same age, who lived at 68 Briar Bank, Carlisle. Keith was exceptionally good looking.

"He was so handsome that when I had to go into into hospital to have children, the nurses were mostly interested, not in patients like me, but in Keith," Stanella said later, "He was so good looking that the nurses couldn`t take their eyes off him."

Back home in Petteril Bank, Stanella and Keith were known as the most handsome couple in the area.

The wedding witnesses at the Carlisle Register Office ceremony on February 25 1950 were her brother Brian and a long-standing friend, Dorothy Cornthwaite. Surprisingly, Stanella was described on the marriage certificate as a machinist at the Carlisle Metal Box factory, a job she never mentioned later in life.

The marriage like her birth was to be a testing time for her father and mother. And it was to be traumatic for Stanella. .

It was not only Keith`s good looks that attracted her. Keith was known to the family through his engine cleaner`s job - the same job her father Jimmy had before he was promoted to fireman. The two men worked together from time to time.

Keith had been clever at school and wanted to be an architect. But that job involved an apprenticeship on a low wage. He couldn`t take up that apprenticeship because his family needed him on a much bigger wage.

How Stanella and Keith actually got together was easily explained, according to Stanella many years later. She recalled: "I had a date with someone else and was on my way when I ran into Keith. He had some cigarette cards and said to me:`Would you like to have a look at these?` "I said I would and that was that. I never went on the date but went with Keith and his cigarette cards and I stuck with him from that time until we were married."

The planned marriage proved to be a worry for Stanella`s mum and dad. The couple had still not told her the truth of her birth and her upbringing in the Henderson household. Stanella`s birth had been registered as the daughter of Anne Clenaghan. Bessie and Jimmy were worried that when the registration of the marriage took place, that birth information might be produced for all the world to see.

If that had happened, of course, it would have been a disaster for Jimmy and Bessie who were still apparently unable to bring themselves to tell Stanella about her background. How Stanella would have reacted if the truth had come out is imposible to guess.

But that "disaster" at the marriage registration was avoided. How, is not clear. But many years afterwards,Stanella became convinced that the half dozen or so other people present at Carlisle Register Office knew the truth about her birth when they came to witness the signing of the marriage certificate. The signing went without a hitch with Stanella marrying, not in her biological name of Clenaghan but in the name of Henderson, the name she had always been known by.

Eight years later, when she was finally told the truth about her background, she recalled the atmosphere at the marriage signing and had this to say: "I sensed there was something unusual going on while the signing took place. Particularly odd was the behaviour of the registrar. He had a big piece of blotting paper which he used to keep covering up everything as the signing went along."

"Whether the registrar was in the know about my birth and what followed is of course impossible to say. If he was in the know, he must have been briefed about it beforehand by someone in the family because it was was impossible for him to know about it without some briefing."

Surprisingly, there was one person who was apparently briefed beforehand about Stanella`s birth and upbringing in the Henderson household. That person was bridegroom Keith. Like other people in the know, Keith had apparently been instructed by Bessie and Jimmy to keep everything secret. And keep everything secret, Keith did until eight years into the marriage. And then, the whole sorry saga came out …deception…secrecy… and cover up… deception…secrecy… and cover up…

How everything unravelled and the "secret" came out seems inevitable, looking back several decades later. The saga of Stanella`s illegitimacy of course most likely had its origins in Stanella`s mother, Anne, in a secret love affair. But no record exists of such an affair. And none of Anne`s relatives I have asked has any idea who Stanella`s father might be.

But the story was later told of Ann`s "secret pregnancy." Stanella got it from Anne`s sister Margaret a year or two before Margaret`s death. The pregnancy was followed by Stanella`s "secret" birth….many miles from her parents` home, and then the "secret" giving away of Stanella to Bessie and Jimmy Henderson which was accompanied by the"secret"naming of her with the Henderson family name. Finally, when Stanella got married she was still not told of her birth and her real mother.

Most people would understand Anne Clenaghan`s "deception," bearing in mind the stigma at that time of illegitimacy and Anne`s father`s local prominence as a businessman, added to his strong religious views and religious connections. Most people would also understand the Henderson family`s"deception," bearing in mind their problem in adopting Stanella and their ever-present fear that, because they had no legal hold over her, she could suddenly be taken away from them by her mother, Anne. Bessie and Jimmy Henderson had many days, months, and years of anguish and fear. They said later that on many occasions they wanted to to tell Stanella the truth about her birth. Had they done that, they no doubt would have felt more at ease. But on each occasion they were held back from telling her because they feared a backlash from Stanella which they felt might result in their losing her.

Times of course have changed. Today, there would have been no problems about adoption which no doubt in this case would have gone ahead. And today there would have been no "secrecy" from then on because Stanella, as soon as she she could understand it, would have been told the truth of her birth. It now seems to be generally accepted that children should be told of their adoption as early as possible.

Stanella was to be well into her twenties before the "secret" was out. By then, she and Keith had three children, Elaine, Bryan and Keith and were living in a rented railway house in Hasell Street, a few streets away from Ridgemount Road. It was a hard time for the family as they struggled on Keith`s low wages to furnish the house and to have enough to live. Much of the house remained unfurnished. And there were rats.

Stanella afterwards said they suffered because they were so poor. For example, their children had no costumes for swimming lessons at school and had to borrow these from their friends. The three children's names were read out at school among all the others who qualified for free school meals because their parents could not afford them. That was embarrassing for the three .

Sometimes if there was not enough money to feed all the family, Stanella had to go hungry. Sometimes there was no money at all from husband Keith for whatever reason, and for a week they had to scrape along as best they could. When the rentman was due, the family put out the lights to indicate there was no one at home.

But Bessie and Jimmy were very supportive with gifts of cash and food. Stanella eventually came to realise that they had been too young to marry and have a family - both were still teenagers - on Keith's low wages.

Possibly, with the strain of the struggle, things eventually came to head with a row between the two of them. What the row was all about is now long forgotten but in the course of it, Stanella threw her wedding ring into the kitchen fire and then told Keith that she would "tell my mam" all about it.

What she planned to tell her mam has been long forgotten. But what followed was disastrous for both Stanella and Keith and their three children.

THE STORY STARTS TO UNRAVEL

Stanella takes up the story several years later: "When I mentioned `mam,' Keith replied, `You will have a hard job to tell your mam.' "I said: `No I won`t. I will just go and tell her now.' So I got my coat and made for the door. Keith said: "It`s no use going to tell Bessie, because Bessie is not your mam." I couldn`t believe what I was hearing, I was so shocked.

"I was sobbing. I got hold of Keith and shook him to get him to repeat what he had said and to get him to explain that my mam wasn`t my mam. Then it all came out that she and my dad had brought me up but I wasn`t their child. "I have never felt so unhappy. I couldn`t stop sobbing. I grabbed my coat and set off running for my mam`s house in Ridgemount Road. I didn`t know what I was doing or what I was going to say, I was so confused.

"When I got to Ridgemount Road, I realised that my dad would also be at home. That thought made it worse

No father`s name- Stanella`s birth certificate.

because I didn't want to upset both of them, particularly as my dad would be going to work in the morning. When I got to the house, I just didn't know what to do, I was so upset. I wanted to knock on the door but decided not to. I was shaking very much. So I decided to go into the outside toilet and collect my thoughts and wait in the hope that my dad might go to work at some time during the night as he often did. I waited and waited in the hope that he would leave the house. But he never moved until morning. I had been there all night. It was very very cold and I was crying most of the time because I was deeply unhappy. I have no idea how I put in the hours until I heard my dad leave the house and go to work. I crept out and let myself into the house. Mam was in the kitchen and could see that I was dreadfully upset.

Somehow she knew exactly what had happened. She said "Oh lass, has he gone and told you?" All I could do was to tell her the story of the row and tell it again and again, sobbing all the time. "I said 'Mam, I have never ever thought of you as anyone but my Mam and I never will. I love you so much.'

"Mam said that my dad, Jimmy had for a long time had wanted to tell me but she wouldn't let him. "She said: `I have never known what to do for the best. At first I didn't want to tell you because I thought I would lose you. `Then I didn't want to tell you because I knew it would upset you and God knows what you would have done. All I wanted to do was to protect you.`"

Stanella never returned to Keith. Nor did she ever return to the house in Hasell Street. All her clothes and other possessions were left there. Keith tried many times to get her to return but each time she refused. Paradoxically, when a special effort was made at a magistrates` court to get the couple together again, Stanella agreed to a new start, but Keith said: "I want my freedom."

Afterwards he regretted what he had said. However, the marriage was finished. It had failed. The couple divorced and Keith went on to re-marry and have another family. But every year afterwards until he died he sent Stanella a "mystery" valentine card signing it "Adorjan," thought to be a Polish name.

Why had the marriage failed? Stanella always agreed that she and Keith had been too young to marry and that could have been responsible for the failure. But she also had another explanation. This was that her life had been changed irrevocably since she discovered that Bessie Henderson was not her real mother and Jimmy Henderson was not her real father.

And that change meant that she could not go back to being married to Keith. She would say: "I sometimes feel complete helpless wondering about my real father and mother and not getting any answers. I used to go into the centre of Carlisle just to look at the faces of the people there to see if I could find any face similar to my own that might lead me to my real father."

Then I would go off on another track and think that Jimmy Henderson, the man I called Dad, might be my real father. "I was very troubled by it all and often felt disconnected from reality." Stanella continued to live with her mam and dad and brought her three children to live with her there. It was to be the start of a second life at Ridgemount Road.

That second life lasted three years and was not easy for the two families, somewhat cramped in a three-bedroom house, which was designed for only one family. Sadly during the three years, in 1961, Stanella's father Jimmy died from a heart attack. He had just returned home during the early hours after driving an express train 300 miles from London and was making himself a pot of tea when he collapsed and died in the kitchen. He was not found until the next morning. The kettle was burned through. He was 59.

His death eased the strain in the house but it meant that the principle income had gone. Stanella's brother Roy became the breadwinner and "father" to Stanella's children. These new responsibilities Roy gladly accepted until Bessie's death ten years later. By then Stanella had remarried but she was eternally grateful to Roy and Bessie for their love and support. She was able to return a little of that love and support by inviting them every week for a meal in her new home.

A DENTIST FROM THE ISLE OF MAN

There was an uncanny story attached to the death of Stanella`s mother, Bessie, eleven years after Jimmy`s death. She was 79 and had been failing in health for several weeks. Unknown to her, an elderly man in the Isle of Man wanted to see her, although he knew nothing of her failing health.

His name was Harry Black, a dentist on the island who came to know Bessie Gill, as she was then known, more than fifty years earlier. He was then an injured soldier from the First World War trenches, recovering at Fusehill Hospital in Carlisle which is now the campus of Cumbria University.

Bessie visited Harry in the hospital - it was near the Gill family home in Charles Street - as he recovered from his wounds. The two became friends. After the war they kept in touch with each other by letter, every Christmas, but they never met again, much to Harry`s regret.

However, in 1971, Harry, then in his seventies, decided that he would like to meet Bessie once again. He arranged a flight to Newcastle, managing to get the last seat on a plane. He was greatly elated when he arrived at Carlisle with a few gifts for Bessie and her family. Sad to relate, Harry discovered shorty after arriving that Bessie had just died. The death, by the strangest of coincidences had taken place the previous day.

Harry said later that he never would be able to explain why suddenly after so many years he had felt the need to return to Carlisle. Of course he didn`t know then that Bessie was dying. Afterwards, Harry chatted for hours to members of Bessie`s family before returning to the Isle of Man. He recalled the kindness of Bessie and her family to himself and other wounded soldiers in the Carlisle hospital.

Stanella was happy to join the others who met Harry while at the same time she was recovering from the shock of her mother`s death. She and her brother Roy arranged Bessie`s funeral. Stanella and Roy had both been with Bessie when she died. Bessie kissed both of them and said to each: "You two have been blessings".

Stanella`s loss of her mother was a big blow, but things by then had started to look brighter for her.She had found a new husband and a new home. The lucky man was myself, John Barker, a Carlisle freelance journalist and businessman. Stanella and I met at a Tuesday night dance at the County Hotel in the centre of the city.

I well remember the meeting- Stanella was wearing a white blouse and a stunning flowing red skirt - she called it a bullfighter skirt. Stanella looked her best in red but it was colour she shied away from, always going for her favourite colour, blue. I was 32 and Stanella was 28 and there seemed to be an almost instant attraction between us. Stanella said the chemistry was good.

Certainly there was something positive going on because that meeting rapidly developed into a meeting every day and a letter every day and it was soon decided to get engaged if that was possible. But possible it was not. Stanella was still married to Keith, although the two had lived apart for three years.

So Stanella decided to sue for a divorce and plans were made to marry on Stanella`s twenty eighth birthday at the city register office. The divorce came through and I  paid £3,750 for a four-bedroom detached house, named Lyncroft, in Durranhill Road - later renamed Harraby Grove - an easy walking distance from Stanella`s family home in Ridgemount Road.

Sadly, the house I bought had to remain unoccupied for nearly a year because we decided not to move in until we were married. The house was also near the children`s schools and of course handy for Stanella`s mother and brother Roy who became visitors every week. The house was built twenty years earlier by a Mr North, the boss of the city co-op and, according to Stanella, the house was one-up on all other houses in the area.

Why was it one-up? Because it was built with Accrington Brick, an expensive polished brick and a feature of the house which Stanella never tired of boasting about. All the houses in that part of Durranhill Road were different, all apparently architect - designed to the wishes of different middle class families. Lyncroft was unusual in that it had a separate rose garden complete with sundial and also a separate small orchard.

Before the Second World War, Durranhill Road was surrounded by fields. A couple of decades later, when we moved on to the road, it was surrounded by the newly completed Harraby council housing estate where 10,000 people lived. At one end of Durranhill Road, about 100 yards from our home was the Harraby Inn, a state managed pub once the home of the Cavaghan family who ran a big and well-known Carlisle meat processing and manufacturing company.

State managed pubs as I mentioned earlier had been a feature of Carlisle life since 1916 when the all the pubs were nationalised by David Lloyd George. The Harraby Inn was the "local" of Stanella`s father Jimmy and her three brothers. Jimmy played bowls on the pub`s bowling green, sang Danny Boy in the bar whenever he felt like it, and at 2 pm closing time on a Sunday would arrive home from the pub carrying a large block of ice cream for the family.

Opposite the Harraby Inn was a large older house, the home of the Frasers, a well-known Carlisle family of doctors. One of that family was George MacDonald Fraser, who later achieved fame as an author and screenwriter, best known for his best selling Flashman books. George was brought up in Currock, a quarter of a mile away and in his younger days was a frequent visitor to his relatives in Durranhill Road. He started his working life as a Carlisle journalist and later was a wartime Scottish infantry officer and an author.

Before our wedding, Stanella managed to get to know the staff of Border Press Agency, a provincial news agency run by myself and my brother Peter. The agency was based in Lonsdale Street in the city centre. Stanella also travelled to Keswick where I was born and brought up to meet my mother, Kate, a widow living alone in Ambleside Road.

The two women got on well but Kate decided to give the wedding a miss and instead went to stay with a friend in the south of England. That decision was very disappointing but not surprising. Disappointing, because of Kate`s absence other family members also decided to stay away. It was not surprising, because my very religious mother - a devoted member of the Plymouth Brethren - was firmly against divorce and even more firmly against her son marrying a divorced woman, particularly a divorced woman with three children. She never voiced any opposition to the wedding and very soon afterwards became very kind to Stanella and myself. And as a help to becoming friends again she became heavily engaged in buying furniture and other items for our house, Lyncroft.

NO SECRETS AT THIS WEDDING

Second wedding - Stanella with husband John Barker, best man Peter Barker and matron of honour, Kathleen Barker .

33

Our wedding took place as planned at 11 am on Stanella`s birthday, November 29 1961. (My father, Adam, had the same birthday). My late brother Peter was best man and Peter`s wife Kathleen, matron of honour. Kathleen and Peter, both of them already great friends and colleagues, were the greatest support to both of us that day. They since continued their great friendship and support until Peter`s death in 2021 at the age of 89.

We all enjoyed the wedding day and afterwards noted with quiet satisfaction that unlike Stanella`s first wedding, everything had been very open and transparent when it came to the signing of the documents after the ceremony. There had been no "manoeuvring with blotting paper" by the registrar in order apparently to hide "secrets" of Stanella`s birth. These birth details were secret no longer.

The wedding reception consisted of a "wedding present" meal for the four of us at the Silver Grill, a leading city centre restaurant, now the site of Boots the chemist. The meal was a gift from the Silver Grill manager, Ray Taylor, a friend of Stanella and myself. A honeymoon abroad- fairly rare at that time - was planned and Peter and Kathleen saw us off on the train for London, bound for Heathrow and Majorca. There were no direct flights to Majorca in those days. We did the flight in two hops, changing planes at Barcelona.

It was an unsettled time for Stanella at one stage of the journey.She became very disorientated during the night of our overnight stay at a Heathrow hotel. She suddenly woke up in her sleep, calling for her brother Roy thinking she was back in Ridgemount Road in Carlisle. Once woken up, she was convinced she had failed to waken Roy as she had done every morning for some years.

The fortnight in Majorca was booked at the five-star Victoria Hotel in Palma where there were four waiters to every table. It was there we met up with another Cumbria honeymooning couple. Ormond and Barbara Holiday came from the Silloth area, just a few miles from Carlisle, and had been married near their home on the same day as ourselves.

All the luxury of the Victoria Hotel brought on bouts of guilt for Stanella when she recalled her previous somewhat cramped life back in Ridgemout Road, and the rat infested house in Hasell Street where she lived during her previous marriage. She badly missed her children, but we enjoyed the November sunshine, loved swimming in the sea, and never tired of taking bus rides and car rides along the Palma seafront. Stella had never learned to swim, but she tried hard to keep up with my swimming.

When we returned to Carlisle we renewed our Majorca honeymoon friendship with Ormond and Barbara Holiday and were once entertained at their home for dinner. By coincidence twenty or so years later, our daughter Alyson met up several times with the Holiday`s dashing son, Johnny, who had become a pilot.

Newlyweds take time to adjust to each other and it was much the same with us in our new home, Lyncroft. The children, Elaine, 11, Brian, 8, and Keith, 6, were also part of the adjusting. It all seemed to go well at the start and all except Keith settled down to a new routine.

Keith decided on the first day that life in Durranhill Road was not for him. He got his overcoat and announced: "I am going back home to my Nana`s." It was only after a lot of persuading that he reluctantly decided to stay and accept that he now had a new home.

Stanella`s new life with me was not easy. She soon found that she had to play an important role in my growing Carlisle news agency business of collecting news and sending it to national and provincial newspapers.

The agency was started about three years earlier after I moved to Carlisle from Manchester where I had been working as a sub editor on the Daily Express and on another daily newspaper, the News Chonicle. Previously I had worked as reporter and a sub editor on the Salisbury Journal, the Penrith Observer, the Cumberland News the Sunderland Echo, the Shields Gazette, the Evening Chronicle, Newcastle and the Journal, Newcastle. In a badly-advised move when I was 26 I started my own weekly newspaper, the Wallsend Observer which ran for just seven issues. I was much more successful twenty years later with Lakescene, a monthly magazine which I started and ran for several years.

Stanella`s role was mainly manning the phone at home after hours i.e. whenever the news agency`s office was closed and newspapers or business contacts wished to get in touch with me. Many messages had to be taken every week and many calls re-directed. Stanella had little previous experience of the telephone - neither of her previous homes had telephones - but she soon adapted to her new role. What was far more difficult was adapting to my very irregular lifestyle as a freelance journalist and businessman.

She did try very hard to make things work between us. But as time went on, her lovely evening meals which she invariably had ready for 6 pm were becoming increasingly postponed to later times because I was at the office working, sometimes to 8 pm. These were the days before microwave ovens which today are often indispensible to wives wishing to warm up a meal.

I always had a reason for not arriving for my evening meal on time. That reason usually was that I had been delayed in the office by a late breaking item of news that had to be dealt with there and then with all the urgency that competitive news gathering demanded. I had an increasingly growing business but I knew it was only growing because of my dedication to the day to day leadership in the running of affairs. There was always the possibility that business rivals would get in front with a quicker news gathering operation. And that could never be allowed to happen.

For Stanella, my continued lateness for meals meant increased inconvenience in the running of the home and an unsettled marriage in which she was seeing less and less of her husband. She often failed to see my reason for the increasingly long hours of working and frequently told me so. And she also constantly told me that she failed to see why it was her husband who always had to work late and not one of his employees.

Long hours and late meals became a stalemate situation and the cause of much friction between us. The situation was not helped by a miscarriage about a year after our marriage. Fortunately to our great joy, Stanella became pregnant again about a year later and Alyson was born. Alyson got her name from Alyson Tinning, an outstandingly attractive woman who Stanella knew. Alyson was given Anne as a second name.

Alyson's christening.

Anne as it happened was also the name of Stanella`s birth mother, but at that time this apparent connection had not been discovered by Stanella.

A new baby for Stanella, which of course added to her family of three children, meant that she had an increasingly busy life in her new home In Durranhill Road.

Lyncroft was a much bigger house than Stanella had ever been used to but she was very fortunate in one respect. Because of her very warm personality, she quickly made friends with the neighbours.

In return for that friendship she got a lot of backing and friendliness from the same neighbours who proved to be a group of very friendly and supportive people.

Next door neighbour was Mrs Glaister - we never knew her christian name - an elderly widow living alone. She appeared very lonely, and loved nothing more than coming into our house, joining Stanella in the kitchen and making meals for our family.

We, in return, invited Mrs Glaister to join us on

family car trips. One memorable trip was to Edinburgh Zoo.

When Stanella had to leave our house to have baby Alyson, Mrs Glaister lost no time in taking her place in the Lyncroft kitchen and very lovingly made our family meals and generally looked after things. She appeared to be very upset when, after three days, Stanella appeared at the door of Lyncroft with the baby. Mrs Glaister`s first words to Stanella were in mock protest at her return home. She said: "No, you`re not coming in. Get away back to where you have been. We have managed quite well without you." The episode was a good laugh for all of us. And it still is a good laugh when we recall it.

Another good laugh came with an elderly gardener, David Griffiths who worked part time for Mrs Glaister. He was in his seventies but spent a lot of his working time romancing Mrs Glaister who, he declared, he planned to marry. But she was having none of it. She explained to Stanella and I why she kept turning him down. This to and fro between the two of them became an almost daily commentary.

Sadly, Mrs Glaister developed dementia some years later and ended her life in a care home. Her start in life had been far from happy, as she recalled several times to Stanella and I. She had been brought up by an aunt at Eamont Bridge, near Penrith and as a baby and a toddler had regularly been fed an opium drug, all apparently done quite legally. The drug was laudanum.

Laudanum was spoon fed by nurses and baby-minders to put babies and infants to sleep. This enforced sleep enabled the nurses and others to neglect their duties if they so wished. At that time, laudanum was available at chemists and other shops. Now its sale is greatly restricted and has to be labelled "Poison."

COFFEE AND BISCUITS AT TEN O CLOCK

Joan Buet, another neighbour, was a daily ten o`clock visitor to our house for coffee and biscuits. She and her husband Frank and their three children, like Mrs Glaister, were the friendliest and kindest people. The Buets could always be found ready and able to help if some problem arose. Frank, an army captain during the Second World War, was a property expert working for an international tyre company.

The family moved to Durranhill Road from Plymouth shortly after Stanella and I arrived on the road. Frank was also a city councillor. Sadly he died following a massive heart attack on the doorstep of his home.

Joan came from a long-living family. Her mother was 104 when she died, very dramatically, as it happened, in Stanella`s arms. Stanella had taken the old lady to the Cumberland Infirmary in Carlisle for an examination, Stanella was standing in for Joan who was away on holiday at the time. The old lady was in a wheelchair and she and Stanella were waiting to be seen in an infirmary corridor. Without any warning, the old lady collapsed and died.

Joan has now lived nearly as long as her mother. She had no difficulty in sailing past 100. She is now 103 and after living with her daughter in the Midlands recently moved into a care home. Two other neighbours, Brian Neil and his wife Rose also lived opposite us on Durranhill Road. They were from Larne in Northern Ireland. Brian worked as an odd job man at the nearby Border Television studios. Rose had a fashion business in the city.

The couple, like Joan and Frank and Mrs Glaister were kind and supportive. Rose had tried repeatedly to become pregnant only to have a miscarriage each time. She and Brian doted on our children much more than most people, possibly because, sadly, they were denied children. Brian was a great do-it-yourself enthusiast and there was little of their bungalow that he had not altered over the years.

Rose used to joke about this. She said that the do it yourself alterations were so extensive that she often feared that the bungalow would collapse. Rose spent many hours accompanying Stanella as she learned to drive. Sadly it was time spent in vain because Stanella never managed to get as far as the driving test.

Rose and Brian returned to Ireland shortly after our family left Lyncroft for a new house at the other end of the city. The move was to prove disastrous for Stanella. Before I describe that disaster let me tell you of some of the other families in Durranhill Road which we got to know. All of them had interesting stories.

Possibly the most colourful was a middle aged woman who turned up up at one of our family weddings although she hadn`t been invited. She joined the guests after the ceremony at the meal at our home afterwards. Then she said: "Can I do you a favour by helping with the washing up?"

Help she did and when the washing up was finished, she continued to stay for later celebrations. Of course we thought her behaviour very strange. Later we learned that this was not the first wedding she had gatecrashed and turned up to uninvited. Over the years she had gained a reputation in the city for turning up at weddings in this way. She could, I suppose, be described as a professional wedding guest. Sadly, she was left destitute when the man she was living with died. In his will he left their house and all his money to his wife who he had left many years earlier. We never learned how she coped.

Another neighbour was a man who sunbathed in the nude in his garden. Another was an alcoholic who sometimes could be seen in his garden, hiding drink under plant pots! One neighbour had 15 Shetland Sheepdogs (Shelties)... they drowned out everything when they barked together and sadly they became a nuisance.

STANELLA'S FAMILY OF FIVE

Let me now tell you more about Stanella`s children.

Elaine, the eldest, wanted to become a nurse and succeeded in getting a place at Newcastle City General Hospital for her training.She continued nursing in Newcastle then worked in London where at one time she nursed Shirley Bassey. She went on to marry but kept up with her nursing. Because she and her husband were unable to have children, they adopted a boy and a girl, Adam and Charlotte. Elaine now has four grandchildren. She and her husband Andy, a retired Church of Scotland minister live in Glasgow. Adam is an pilot, currently a first officer with Tui Airlines. Charlotte works for the Victoria and Albert Museum and is is senior curator at V and A Dundee. Stanellla`s elder boys, Bryan and Keith, both passed the eleven plus examination which gave them places at Carlisle Grammar School. Keith was his year`s top eleven plus winner in the city of Carlisle. Both brothers were also chosen for Carlisle Cathedral Choir where Keith became head boy. Their record with the choir was excellent, both showing great dedication. Dedication was not easy. Choir boys as young as seven or eight were expected to sing in the choir every day after school and twice on a Sunday. That routine lasted for several years and only ended when their voices broke.

Cathedral choirboy Bryan, Stanella's son with her mother Bessie.

Bryan went on have his own one-man transport business which he ran until his retirement. He lives in Carlisle and never married.

Keith worked for only one company throughout his working life in which at 65 he was still active. He retired this year after completing half a century with that company. It was an enviable record.

He joined the Post Office on the telephone side when he left school and when that side of the organisation became British Telecom he continued in a telecom job, gaining promotion to a management auditing position.

He and his wife Linda who live in Carlisle have three children, Lucy, Felicity and Robin, and four grandchildren.

Jonathan, the youngest is four years younger than the late Alyson. He became involved in the trucking business from a very early age because of his fondness for a trucking company which was based a stone`s throw from our home.

Robson`s Border Transport had nearly 200 vehicles and from the age of about six, there was nothing Jonathan enjoyed more than playing among the Daf trucks, the Leylands and the Seddon Atkinsons based at Robson`s. Robson`s trucks were not your ordinary run-of-the-mill vehicles. All had a different Border name, Border Raider, and Border Diamond were examples. And all stood out from other trucks in an easily recognisable and distinctive cream and maroon livery. Robson`s were pioneers in standardising their vehicles in this distinctive way, and were closely followed by many other trucking companies, notably the nationally recognised company, Eddie Stobart. Jonathan worked for Stobarts some years later.

As Jonathan grew older he managed to get free truck rides with many of the drivers and prior to leaving school he spent every Friday night travelling 200 miles in a Robson`s lorry cab to Sandbach in Cheshire and back again to Carlisle. The lorry driver, Willie Keen made the same trip every Friday night and four other nights every week

One story illustrates just how devoted Jonathan was to trucking. When he was about eight years old, he gave some thought about his Dad`s job - my job as a journalist. He decided that his Dad had a very boring office job and would be much happier with an exciting job. That job, he decided, was driving a Robson`s truck.

So he resolved to get his Dad a job working at Robson`s, where he spent many hours of his free time. He made contact with the Robson bosses, who he already knew, and explained that he wanted a lorry driver`s job for his Dad. Whether the bosses took him seriously or not, I cannot recall. But he was told to send his Dad for an interview.

How to get his Dad to that interview was a problem. But Jonathan persevered and, more to keep the peace than anything, I gave in and agreed to go along to the Robson`s depot and be "interviewed." Needless to say, I never got the job. But the Robson bosses played along very well with the pretend interview and I was told at the end of the ten minutes with them that I was both too old for the job and completely unskilled in lorry driving!.

Sadly, with regret they said, they had to turn me down! Jonathan`s long interest in trucks continued to the end of his schooldays and it followed naturally that he got a job as an an apprentice mechanic with a Carlisle truck maintainance company, Solway Daf. That job was followed by the truck driving job with Eddie Stobart which was an up and coming company that came to be very well known throughout the country. Many people considered Eddie Stobart a worthy successor to Jonathan`s first love, Robson`s Border Transport.

Stobart`s job lasted for 21 years and involved driving in this country and all over Europe. Jonathan ended up as one of Stobart executives. For the last 14 years Jonathan has run Leisurematic, a business he himself started. The business now claims to be the leading kiddie ride and amusement machine supplier in the country. He lives in Carlisle and is married to Aileen and has two teenaged daughters, Kirstie and Hannah.

All three boys, Bryan, Keith and Jonathan as they grew up spent time with me while I did my job as a journalist in and around Carlisle. Sometimes one of them came with me to a meeting and sometimes they joined me at a football match. It was on one of those occasions that Jonathan met the then Prime Minister, Mr Harold Wilson. Jonathan was then aged about three and was with me shopping on a Saturday afternoon in Carlisle city centre.

Mr Wilson was on a visit to the city and I decided to find out if there was a newspaper story in his visit. So Jonathan and I made our way to the city Civic Centre. There we bumped into the city`s Labour MP, Mr Ron Lewis, who I knew well through my job. Mr Lewis was his usual friendly self and was soon chatting to Jonathan who at the time I was carrying. Mr Lewis suggested that Jonathan might like to meet the prime minister who we were told was upstairs. We were pleasantly surprised at this and naturally agreed.

No sooner said than done. Mr Lewis turned on his heels, marched to the bottom of the Civic Centre stairs and shouted up to the next floor;"Harold! Come downstairs and meet Jonathan." Again, no sooner said than done. Mr Wilson, complete with his trademark pipe and Gannex raincoat duly appeared on the stairs and made his way to the three of us, Mr Lewis and myself carrying Jonathan.

Mr Wilson was soon into a conversation with Jonathan lasting two or three minutes asking him how old he was, where he had been that day and where he now planned to go. It was very pleasant surprise encounter for Jonathan and myself which Jonathan still happily remembers. We also remember the day for another reason: it was also Stanella`s fortieth birthday.

A few years later, when Jonathan was twelve he decided to write letter to the Carlisle newspaper, The News and Star. The first we heard of the letter was when it was published under the headline: "Why my mum`s best." The letter said: "I think my mum`s is the greatest because she bothers to get up in the morning and make my breakfast and if it is anybody`s birthday or at Christmas she will spend every last penny on you to make it a happy occasion and she shares everything she has got with you. And she always gets my favourite food and I think she deserves some flowers."

Prior to Jonathan`s birth, all our family was presented to the people of Carlisle in two very large newspaper advertisements. These were part of a local promotion for milk. Our part in the promotion came about because we were good customers of our milkman who in those days delivered his bottles by horse and cart. To our surprise in 1966 we were chosen to appear in the two full page advertisments in the Carlisle local daily newspaper, the Cumberland Evening News, now called the News and Star.

The first advert, which included one of the pictures, was headed: "Pinta families in Cumberland- you can tell them by their doorsteps."

PINTA FAMILIES IN CUMBERLAND

The Pinta family- Stanella and John with Bryan(left), Elaine(centre), Keith and Alyson(front).

The advert went on: "Pinta families are those that take a pint of milk for every member every day." Then the advert went on as follows to list all members of our family:

"Mr John Barker is a journalist. He likes his milk flavoured with a meat cube and enjoys his wife`s cooking in which she uses plenty of milk. Elaine is 16. She has a job in an office, likes to drink her milk in coffee and is all for creamy milk puddings. Bryan, 13, is at grammar school, mad on horses and rugger, sings in the Cathedral choir, and likes to drink his milk cold, lots of it."

"Keith is 10 and another keen milk drinker- in fact they have to hide it from him! He`s at junior school and also sings in the Cathedral choir. It looks like they`re going to have another journalist in the family, for in the holidays Keith often helps in the office. Alyson, aged 3 is a keen cyclist (on three wheels). She loves milk drinks of all kinds which no doubt has a lot to do with her bonny looks."

"Mother, Mrs Stella Barker is as full of life and energy as the rest of the family. She believes in milk, believes that every penny of the milk bill is well spent because it buys real food value. Especially in winter, for milk helps to build up the family`s resistance to colds and flu."

The second advertisement, which included the second family picture, appeared the following year and was headed: "What a pinta family is...and why you should be one too!" This was followed by several paragraphs extolling the health values of milk. The two pinta adverts brought the family a lot of publicity and there was a lot of good-humoured banter from neighbours and friends. This went on for months afterwards.

There was banter too at our home, not because of pinta advertisement but because of a bird, a jackdaw! It was a young bird that had fallen from its nest and was brought home by Bryan, a great bird lover. He fed it with scraps and often Stanella joined in.

The bird thrived on good food and lots of love and it soon became a family pet we called Jack. It flew round the houses but always returned to our garage where it always was fed. So tame did the bird become that it would respond to the call "Jack" and fly on to the caller`s shoulder. Jack became particularly fond of Stanella and people passing our house would stop to see Jack flying around and then landing on Stanella`s shoulders.

STANELLA'S MOTHER AND HER FAMILY

Stanella`s mother Anne...the very image of her daughter.

Stanella`s biological mother Anne, had three other children following her marriage. Gordon, the first child was born in 1942 at Potters Bar in Hertfordshire, 300 miles away from Carlisle. It was a year after her marriage which also took place at Potters Bar. Anne`s husband, Noel, a mechanical engineer had served in the RAF during the war but when he married he had left the RAF and was Senior Designer at the De Havilland Aircraft Company at nearby Hatfield where he met Anne.

Around the end of the war, in 1944, Noel was appointed chief designer at Portsmouth Aviation, a leading engineering solution provider, where he remained until he retired. The family moved to Portsmouth for this job and initially rented a small semi detached house in the village of Waterlooville where the second son, Ian was born in 1944.

The family then moved to a house in the neighbouring village of Denmead, where their third son Douglas was born in 1950. Around 1956, they moved back to Waterlooville and stayed until 1968. They then moved to a big house in Hayling Island, where they remained until they died. Noel died about 1980 and Anne followed about ten years later.

Noel is stll fondly remembered at Portsmouth Aviation. Simon Escott, the managing director told me in an email: "Noel had a key role in the development in 1947 of our first and only aircraft – the Aerocar - fully manufactured by Portsmouth Aviation. My father, who is now in his late seventies, has mentioned Noel a few times to me in the past, so I know the importance of his role here."

The Aerocar, as its name implies was a dual purpose vehicle designed to act either as a car or a plane. It was developed as a radical aeroplane, commercialially viable, to challenge the cumbersome pre-war aircraft that were available in the 1930s. It never reached its potential because the developers were unable to raise the finance needed. Noel`s role is highlighted in detail in a book Spithead Express published later. Mr Escott sent me a copy of the book.

Anne`s youngest son, Douglas never married and lived alone in the Hayling island house until he died in 2020. Second son, Ian is a mechanical engineer. He and his wife Pam, a nurse, moved to Melbourne in 1977 after Ian had been head hunted for a two year contract. Later, he decided to stay in Australia. Pam continued working as a nurse, and Ian ran a company which designs, builds and installs very large steam raising plant including power stations. The job took him all over the country. The couple have two daughters, five grandchildren and three great grandchildren. They are both happily retired now, Ian playing a lot of golf.

THE FAMILY MANSION IS BLOWN UP

It was in the seventies that Stanella came near to meeting her mother, Anne. That near-meeting came about followed increasing curiosity by Stanella about Anne. She knew from her birth certificate that Anne came from Terregles House near Dumfries and many times she talked vaguely of going to visit the house.

DUMFRIES AND GALLOWAY STANDARD AND ADVERTISER, *April 29, 1961.*

HISTORIC LANDMARK TO DISAPPEAR

A view of Terregles House, a fine old mansion house built in red sandstone.

A feature in Terregles House, which links it with its memorable past, is the coat of arms which adorns the staircase wall. This, the Maxwell coat of arms, will be taken down and given to the Maxwell Memorial Hall, Terregles.

Terregles House demolition sale

Some of the fabric of history will be sold next Saturday when the demolition sale of Terregles House, Dumfries, takes place. And soon thereafter this ancient landmark will disappear.

Terregles House was the home of the celebrated Maxwell family who were at one time loyal supporters of Mary Queen of Scots.

The original building has long since disappeared, and the present mansion house, in thick red sandstone, was built in 1789.

The thud of the auctioneer's hammer will be the last of many strange and foreign noises that have resounded through the ancient building.

Scotland's Stuart Queen made at least two visits to Terregles estate. On the first visit in 1563 there would be gaiety and music when Queen Mary came to Dumfries with her Privy Council and spent a night there.

But there would be sadness and tears on the next visit, five years later, for then Mary was fleeing south after defeat at Langside, and the tragic story of Scotland and the Stuarts was moving into its darkest chapter.

Then the building would hear Calvinistic tones in 1639, when an army of Covenanters, 2000 strong, swept into the area and occupied the estate.

In more modern times, before World War I., the house was owned by Major C. E. Galbraith. At the end of that war the estate was bought by Mr James Clenaghan, the well-known local cattle dealer.

Strange sounds, in a foreign tongue, would again resound from the walls in World War II., for Norwegian troops occupied the house then.

Mr Clenaghan returned to live there after the war, and sold the place to the present owner, Mr William Hodge, Terreglestown, in 1957. For some time now the house has been unoccupied.

Then out of the blue in 1974 came news that Terregles House had been demolished by the owner who had it blown up because it had dry rot. The demolition was captured in spectacular pictures.

The explosion was a big event locally and nationally. The pictures appeared in the national press which Stanella, then 42 years old found fascinating.

She preserved them carefully. Before very long, these pictures set her off on a quest to find her birth mother.

The quest lasted for nearly half a century and at her death at the age of 87, Stanella had stll not found what she had been looking for.

Why that search failed after so long I hope to discuss later in the book. But in that half century of looking for her biological mother she often gave the impression that there was something missing in her life. From time to time she was very unsettled.

That apparent lack of stability may have played a part in her wish to move from Harraby Grove after living there for 20 years.

Stanella herself initiated

the move but soon came to regret it. But it was too late. She realised that she had exchanged a life among a community of friends where she had been very happy, for a community of mainly middle class professional people who were quite happy keeping themselves very much to themselves.

The new home was on the opposite side of the city, a detached house, 69 Longlands Road, built in the 1960`s, and bought for £38,000. No longer was there a neighbour, Joan, calling for a ten o`clock coffee and biscuits, or another neighbour, Rose, inviting her to go for an afternoon drive into town. Longlands Road people she soon discovered were not friendly people. Many of them were snooty people, the sort of people she was not used to. And she was lonely.

That problem wasn`t helped by one neighbour who called to our house to welcome our family to Longlands Road. He expressed the hope that we would be happy living here. Then he added a note of caution.

"On this road we respect each other" he said. "But we don`t go into each other`s houses all the time." The hint of ultra privacy on the road was meant to be helpful. But helpful it wasn`t because Stanella was a naturally friendly person and close friendships with neighbours was something she had enjoyed since she was a tiny girl.

Stanella`s loneliness became depression.

There was only one solution and that was to move back to Harraby Grove or to somewhere near. So, about six weeks after moving in, the house at Longlands Road was put back on the market. Neighbours and friends were very surprised and Stanellla and I were told that we had not given the move a chance. Others advised us that in life it is impossible to go back in time.

That bit of advice proved to be very true because we found it impossible to find a house on the market in the vicinity of Harraby Grove where we had once lived. So, reluctantly, plans to move back to Harraby Grove were ditched and we had to face up to living in "unfriendly" Longlands Road.

NEWS OF A WEALTHY CATTLE DEALER

Stanella` best friend, Shirley had a big role in helping her to ease the move to Longlands Road. Shirley also played an important part in helping Stanella`s hunt for her biological mother.

Shirley`s two sons attended St. Joseph`s College, a Catholic school in Dumfries, over the border in Scotland. What Shirley learned about that school and then passed on to Stanella, was an important early link with Stanella`s mother Anne and with Anne`s father, James Clenaghan, a wealthy cattle dealer. Shirley told Stanella that James had been a notable donor to St Joseph`s College, and arguably the school`s biggest donor. Shirley said that on visits to the school she had come across several references to James and his generous gifts.

That information was enough to stir more curiosity in Stanella`s mind about the Clenaghan family. She chatted endlessly about the Clenaghans to Shirley and to me, but never chatted about them, as far as I can remember, to her Henderson family. News of the demolition of Terregles House, as well as stimulating Stanella`s interest in finding her birth mother, was also, paradoxically, a blow to Stanella.

She thought that any clues in her hunt would have vanished in the demolition. Because the house was demolished, there would be little to see. But her curiosity outweighed all of that and she decided that she would, after all like to see Terregles House or what remained of it. So I took her by car several times, to see Terregles village and what we were told was the site of the demolished big house.

On one occasion she got into conversation with a woman from the village and learned that one or more of the Clenaghan family lived somewhere in Edinburgh, but where in the city the woman had no idea. Stanella`s biological mother Anne was not known to the woman.

That information about Edinburgh again increased Stanella`s curiosity. But it also increased her nervousness about the subject. She was happy to talk about wanting to find out more of her birth family but always appeared too nervous of the consequences of her search to do anything about finding some answers. Finally, in about the year 1980, she asked me to find out if there was any Clenaghans in the Edinburgh telephone book.

I discovered the phone number of someone called Margaret Clenaghan. Both Stanella and I puzzled what to do with that bit of information. So Stanella continued to hesitate in moving forward, nervous about what reception we might get from this Margaret Clenaghan, assuming she was somehow related to Anne Clenaghan. I tried to get Stanella to make a phone call to this Margaret Clenaghan. But the call was too much for her and she excused herself by saying she was too shy to make the attempt.

More hesitation followed, more hesitation lasting many days. Then Stanella seemed to get new courage and asked me to make the call. As tactfully as I could, I explained to a woman who answered that my wife Stanella wished to regain the link with her birth family. I explained that the link was broken about half a century earlier when Stanella was given away.

The woman proved to be Anne`s sister, Margaret who naturally was taken off guard and seemed suspicious. I persevered as tactfully as I could. Margaret seemed very interested in everything I said but appeared very reluctant to say too much. But she was as helpful as I am sure she could be while at the same time being on her guard, I suspected in case I was not a genuine caller and, although I did not know it then, Margaret was in close touch with Stanella`s mother, Anne.

Stanella was very nervous and kept in the background as far as possible. But gradually the tension eased and Stanella was persuaded to come to the phone and soon she and Margaret were chatting in friendly way. Margaret told us she had been a nun but was now retired and living in a flat in Edinburgh. I recall that another woman, who I think was Margaret`s sister Mary, joined in the calls. I learned later that at that time Mary lived with Margaret and died shortly afterwards, aged 67.

By the end of the series of phone calls, the ice was well and truly broken and in the coming weeks Stanella and Margaret enjoyed many happy conversations by telephone. Eventually, Stanella was invited to visit Margaret at her home in Edinburgh and went on to make several visits, each time accompanied by our daughter Alyson who drove her there. On each occasion, the two of them had meal at Margaret`s flat and then drove back to Carlisle.

 Alyson was then working as a sales representative, for the Anglo-Swedish pharmaceutical company Astrazeneca. At that company she had an outstanding record as the company`s top sales representative of the year. For that she was given an unusual and unique prize. That prize reflected the company`s Astrazeneca name and the name`sassociation with the stars. It also featured a famous man, also associated with the stars.

That man was the American astronaut, Neil Armstrong, the first man to land on the moon. Alyson`s sales` prize was a dinner with that celebrated man at an exclusive restaurant in Tenerife. Stanella and all the family felt very proud. Alyson was thrilled. A photo of her with Neil Armstrong at the restaurant was treasured by Stanella and all our family. Neil Armstrong died in 2012, three months to the day after Alyson died.

Alyson`s death aged 48 - in June of that year- was a heavy blow to Stanella and myself.

We had supported her for over a year at our home as she struggled with great pain and discomfort from ovarian cancer while trying to work from home. It was a very distressing, hopeless struggle which Alyson could not win. A couple of days before she died she wrote these moving words in a letter to

One small step..for Stanella`s daughter, Alyson. She meets Neil Armstrong, first man on the moon.

Stanella which she called: "In Life".

"When the last days of innocence were over, and experience began to filter through the hazy clouds around my youth, I realised that life cannot hold all that you expect.

"Perfection is an impossibility, but human nature never changes and there is always hope in the somewhere - buried beneath the deep recesses of all that I have learned and loved and lost.

"Days pass quickly now leaving little time to think about the things that can matter. Maybe that`s better (at least it`s easier).

"I still have dreams, still think of the impossibilities. But I am safe in the knowledge of one very important thing, that to you, mother I will always be the same- through time and distance, tears and laughter.So I can still smile.

"With love, Alyson xxxx

ANNE SHARED THE SECRET WITH SISTER MARGARET

During the visits to Edinburgh, Margaret and Stanella got to know each other very well. The relationship was so close it became more like that of a mother and daughter.From conversations in Margaret`s flat it emerged that Margaret had been in touch with Stanella`s mother, Anne ever since they both left the family home, Margaret to become a nun and Anne to marry and have a family.

Not only that, Margaret shared the "secret" of Stanella`s birth.That "secret," I came to learn many years later had understandably not been shared by Anne with her three children. Whether the"secret" had been shared with her husband Noel, we shall never know. Stanella also learned from her conversations with Margaret that the "secret"of her birth had over the years been very much discussed with Anne.

Margaret had been a missionary in South Africa and Lesotho. She apparently left the church in the 1960`s, after Vatican Two, and moved to Leicester where she became headteacher at a school. Later she became head teacher of St Thomas of Aquin`s School at Edinburgh. When she retired from teaching she moved to her final home in Old Farm Court, Colington Road, Edinburgh.Margaret had been the first person in the family to get a university degree, one awarded by the Open University. She was also a poet, greatly influenced by the Victorian poet and Jesuit priest, Gerard Manley Hopkins.

Stanella`s visits to Edinburgh with Alyson ended when Margaret became ill with cancer. She was living at the Sisters of Mercy St Ann`s Home in Dundee where she died on December 8 1998 aged 83. It appears that she had re-joined the church. Stanella and Alyson travelled for the last time to Edinbugh to attend the funeral on December 14 at Mount Vernon Cemetery, and the Requiem Mass at St Catharine`s Convent Chapel, Lauriston Gardens.

 According to Stanella afterwards, she and Alyson were were "treated like royalty" by the nuns who arranged the funeral and by several members of the Clenaghan family who also attended. Stuart Clenaghan, a nephew of Margaret, was one of those who attended. He told me afterwards in letter:" You can imagine that the news of Stanella`s existence came as a surprise to me, but maybe not to the extent that some might think given the large and complicated family that her birth mother, my Aunt Anne came from.

"I met with Stanella and subsequently with Alyson and was delighted that I had discovered such genuine, interesting and nice relatives! Members of our family were of course curious about Stanella`a background and I was able to give them, some limited information."

Stanella kept to herself some of the things she learned from visits to Margaret and would not speak to me about them. So I don`t know what, if anything, Margaret told her about her mother Anne.But at some point during the time of the trips to Edinburgh, Anne`s name appeared to disappear from the conversations I had with

Mam`s girl-Stanella with daughter Alyson in her twenties .

Stanella. It may be that Anne`s death in 1988 may have taken place not long after Stanella first met Margaret. If that is so, her death would have excused Margaret from any promise to put Stanella in touch with Anne.

I continue to wonder why Margaret never did put Stanella in touch with Anne while Anne was alive? Possibly because of the upset such contact would have caused in Anne`s relationship with her husband and her children. Whatever the reason and whatever other questions might be asked and never answered, this short, but very warm relationship between Stanella and Margaret was abortive as far as getting the truth about Stanella`s birth.

For the umpteenth time in her life, Stanella had been denied the full truth about her mother and her birth. For all that time, Anne appears to have had a happy and secure marriage with three children. Anne was a widow when she died on February 15 1988. In her will, made in May 1985, she she left all her estate of £3,155,580 to be divided equally between her three sons: Gordon Henry Sinclair, Douglas Peter Neil, and Ian Frederick James. I estimate that the estate would today be worth about £10 million.

At the time of her death she was living at Dolmans Farm, Ameysford Road, Farndown, Wimborne, Dorset. She had previously lived at The Priory, Alexandra Avenue, Hayling Island, Hampshire. Gordon also lived at Dolmans Farm. Douglas lived at 18 Fathoms Reach, Hayling Island.

After Margaret`s funeral` in 1998, Stanella made no more trips to Edinburgh but treasured the memories of her time spent in the city. She wrote to the nuns who arranged Margaret`s funeral: "This letter comes from my heart to tell you how touched Alyson and I were at the love and kindness shown to us at the funeral.The welcome we received into your home was quite overwhelming. It is a day that shall remain in my heart for the rest of my life. Aunt Margaret always spoke of you with such love and affection and it was easy to see why she did.

"I feel I have been doubly blessed to have met up with my aunt seven and a half years ago and to have had such a loving relationship. And also to have had such a wonderful Mam and Dad, and three brothers who loved me dearly.Aunt Margaret`s death brought to a close some thoughts about a chapter in my life that might have been. But I was able to tell Margaret how loved and how happy my life has really been and it made her so happy.Thank you a million for love you gave in celebration of Margaret`s life and thank you also for the kindness shown during her long illness."

Before she died, Margaret gave Stanella the metal crucifix she wore as a nun. She hung this above her bed. Stanella also left a batch of greetings cards Margaret had sent her over the years. These were addressed to "My Dear Stella" and sometimes "My Dear Stella and Alyson."

In one she writes: "I remember you both, each day at Christmas, that your lives will develop with all the joy possible".In another, Margaret wonders why Stanella had not been in touch and writes:"I have been thinking of you and praying that if you are ill, you may be soon well and fully recovered. I don`t doubt that your happy outlook on life will do you more good than any other therapy. Alyson will have her experienced eye on you too. You are in my thoughts many times a day and that means also in my prayers"

In a sympathy card following the death of Stanella`s brother Roy, Margaret writes: "You know that really he is freed for joy unending. All the suffering is over and the God of Love has taken him into his keeping. At last he has reached the life we are all made for. I envy him.How happy you must be that you cherished and cared for him all through life and especially in his bleak days when he was ill and unable to communicate. How happy you must also be that his dignity is restored and he is alive as never before. He is closer to you now than he ever was. We are the ones left in blind faith till our moment comes."

In a Christmas card sent after Stanella had an operation, Margaret wrote: "This is a Christmas light after your suffering and darkness. I hope you are getting well again.Lots of love and prayers.

"In a card which was undated, Margaret wrote something that is difficult to understand. She wrote "Anne must love you dearly." The card read as follows: "To Stella My Star…loving thanks for all your loving thoughtfulness during my illness. Ann must love you dearly. Happy, glorious Easter, the time of resurrection. Rather wobbly hands. Much love, Margaret. Love to Alyson. Thanks for all the sweeties".

The difficuly is this: Anne died in 1988, so the card would on the face of it have been written before that date. I am not sure that is correct. My feeling is that it was written much later, not long before to Margaret`s death in 1998 at a time when Margaret was very ill with cancer and because of that Stella and Alyson had stopped their visits.

The "wobbly hands" she mentions and the disjointed nature of the message are clues to all that. And it could be that because of her illness she mistakenly wrote thinking Anne was still alive.Or it could be that because of her Catholic faith Margaret was sure that Anne, despite her death lived on.

In her will, Margaret left Stanella a very unusual gift…what apparently was to have been a special carpet. The carpet when it arrived was so worn that Stanella refused to have it in the house. She was convinced that she had either been given the wrong carpet by mistake or that someone had deliberately kept the right carpet and sent her an inferior substitute. The carpet ended in the rubbish bin.

In later years, Stanella sometimes spoke of conversations she had with Margaret about her life as a nun. Particularly she regretted the fact that as a nun she had never been able to earn any money. As a result, when she came to leave that life she had no money and had to rely on gifts from her family to properly exist.

OTHER FAMILY SUCCESS STORIES

Margaret had been well qualified through her Open University degree.But her sisters and brothers had apparently more success. Her youngest sister Sheila, the only one of the siblings now still alive, became an MBE in 1947 for work in the Women`s Auxiliary Air Force in the Second World War.

Sheila later became an international bridge player, representing her country in international tournaments. She turned 100 in April 2022 and lives in a care home in the south of England. Bridget, the fourth daughter of the family, married Scottish international rugby union player Vincent Henderson. The ceremony, at Dumfries Cathedral took place on February 12 1937 followed by a recepton at Terregles House. Vincent was the third son of a Musselburgh jeweller, Mr J.N.Henderson and Mrs Henderson. Bridget`s sister Pat, the sixth daughter, was bridesmaid

Another relative who has become well known is Roddy Clenaghan, son of Anne`s brother, Freddie who died about 15 years ago. Roddy who is 66 is, of course, Stanella`s cousin. He is a talented painter and musician.Painter of Skies is how Roddy describes himself on his web site.He goes on, "I am a Scottish landscape painter with roots and a home on the Isle of Bute. "Most of my paintings depict the mesmerising coastline of the Western Isles of Scotland, in particular, the Firth of Clyde. Although Bute was where my maternal grandmother hailed from and visited regularly throughout my life, I actually grew up in Dumfries".

Roddy studied drawing and painting at Duncan of Jordanstone College of Art in Dundee before moving to Edinburgh to specialise in design. He is currently Creative Lead at a medium size design and advertising agency, based near Milton Keynes.Roddy says he has come back to painting later in life with an enthusiasm, vigour and eye for detail he brings to all his creative pursuits, of which he says he has many.

One of these pursuits is that of a singer and song writer with his own band which is based at the Cock Inn in Stony Stratford, Buckinghamshire. Associated with this band is an online live guide bringing together the worlds of live music, comedy, theatre and festivals. The guide claims to be the biggest in the UK.

Another cousin of Stanella is Stuart Clenaghan who I mentioned earlier. He is the son of Anne`s brother James who was born in 1912 and served as a navigator in Coastal Command during the Second World War. He rejoined the RAF in the early 1950`s and met and married Mary in Germany. Stuart was born in Rostrop near Bremen in 1958 and their daughters, Jacqueline and Fiona, were born at Ely (Cambs) in the early 1960`s.

Stuart, according to his web site, read Natural Sciences at the University of Cambridge and Industrial Sociology and Economics at Imperial College, London. He spent 23 years in international banking, then became an early stage investor in sustainable forestry and environmental enterprises.

His investments include the largest planted forest company in Uganda, a forest conservation private equity company, and a sustainable forestry management company in Peru. Stuart is also a board member of Botanic Gardens Conservation International, a plant conservation charity based a Kew, working with 800 botanic gardens in many countries, whose work forms the world`s largest plant conservation network.

AN ESCAPE TO SCOTLAND

My long research into Stanella`s biological family began more or less with Terregles House, the historic mansion near Dumfries where the family finally settled after James Clenaghan arrived in 1895 from his home in Northern Ireland.James was 26 when he made the move. It was a move, no doubt to benefit the extensive Irish and Scottish cattle dealing business which he ran with his brothers Hugh and John. But it seems very likely the move to Scotland was also greatly prompted by the Irish political troubles.

James found Scotland to be a safe place to bring up his large family and a safe place for business. But back in Northern Ireland there was no let up in the Irish troubles and it seems that it was inevitable that James`s brothers Hugh and John, like James before them, had to escape from the troubles and the widespread arson and other attacks in order to survive.

Hugh made his escape to Dublin while John, who never married lived in both Northern Ireland and Scotland. But the life-long link of the cattle dealing business continued until their deaths... James and John in Scotland and Hugh in Dublin. John remained a bachelor and died at James`s Terregles House, in November 1947 aged about 93.

So this story of abandoned baby, Stanella, through the three brothers and their cattle dealing business, is a Northern Ireland story, as well as a Scottish and Republic of Ireland story. Finally, it is an English story.

The full story started more than a century earlier with farmer John Clenaghan and his wife Bridget, formerly Flanagan, who lived near the Northern Ireland city of Lisburn.In the late 1800`s they had a family of four: John, Hugh, James and Margaret.It was a staunchly Catholic family, not at all wealthy, the parents earning a living from a farm called Brackenhill. They later moved into Lisburn which then was developing very quickly.

This development was particularly noticeable through the major linen manufacturer, Barbour Threads, founded in 1898, and quickly becoming the largest linen thread mill in the world.This industry brought wealth to the town and many Catholics moved in as many restrictions on them had been removed by their emancipation. For the first time they were able to be on par with Protestants.

Everyone, however, was not happy about that as was proved in the violence that followed. The four Clenaghan siblings became victims of that violence, as I mentioned earlier. But the Clenaghan Northern Ireland story is not all about violence. The family produced a nationally known artist, famous for his friendships with British

prime ministers and senior politicians.

The four siblings were cousins of one of Ireland`s most famous painters (pictured left) Sir John Lavery (1856-1941) who as well as achieving fame as an artist, also taught Sir Winston Churchill to paint. Sir John lived in the village of Aghalee in County Antrim on the main road between Lurgan and Antrim, 13 kilometres west of Lisburn. His home is now a restaurant and small hotel named Clenaghans.

Sir John probably became acquainted with Churchill just before and during the First World War when he did a portrait of the famous statesman. That portrait was later hung in Churchill`s home, alongside portraits of some of Churchill`s ancestors.The historian Andrew Roberts in his recent biography of Churchill quotes the great man as saying he took up painting as a form of therapy. Churchill is quoted by Roberts as saying: "If it weren`t for painting, I could not bear the strain of things."

Churchill later wrote: "Painting is complete as a distraction. I know of nothing, without exhausting the body, that more completely absorbs the mind." Churchill was ultimately to paint more than 540 canvasses and became very good indeed, says Roberts. He gave away most of what he modestly called his "daubs" to family and friends and occasionally to other world statesman." Had Churchill chosen painting instead of statesmanship" said Sir John Lavery quoted by Roberts," I believe he would have become a great master with the brush." Lavery was also friendly with Herbert Asquith, British prime minister from 1908-16.

After the First World War, Lavery received a knighthood. In 1921 he was elected to the Royal Academy.

He painted numerous portraits of Irish leaders and after the death of the republican leader Michael Collins, he completed the well-known oil on canvas, Michael Collins "Love of Ireland."

The highest price paid at auction for a painting by Lavery was in 2007 when the impressionist painting, The Bridge at Grez (left) was sold at Christies, London for £1,321,500.

Much memorabilia of the Clengahan-Lavery connection is on display at the Clenaghans restaurant and hotel.

A MURDER BY AMERICAN SOLDIERS.

Clenaghans hit the headlines again eighteen months after Sir John`s death in 1941. A barman at the hotel, a Clenaghan relative, was murdered by two American soldiers. The date was September 21 1942, about ten months after the Japanese attack on Pearl Harbour which sparked America`s entry into the Second World War on the side of the allied countries.

At about that date, American soldiers were starting to arrive in Britain as part of the Allied Forces` build-up for the invasion of France which was planned to follow.There was a camp in Northern Ireland for some of these Americans. It was at Deer Park on the Soldierstown Road at Aghalee, not far from the Clenaghan`s public house.This pub had become favourite spot for the American soldiers to relax every evening.

On the night of September 21, thirty years old Edward Clenaghan was serving in the bar and his brother James, a farmer, was one of the customers. As was usual, the customers included a contingent of American soldiers.Problems arose at closing time when the Americans refused to leave the bar. After a lot of persuasion, all of them except two did eventually leave. The two were Embra H. Farley from Arkansas who was 20 and 26 year old Herbert Jacobs from Kentucky.

More persuasion followed and eventually the two did leave and the bar was closed. But there was more trouble to come. Soon afterwards, the window of the bar was smashed. James went outside to investigate and found the two Americans still demanding more beer. James returned to the bar and Edward said he would go to the Deer Park camp and speak to the commanding officer. He got on his cycle but was soon again confronted by the two Americans. They attacked him and beat him with a steel helmet.

Some time later, James found him lying unconscious at the side of the road. He died the following day in Lurgan Hospital. One of the two Americans stole Edward `s cycle which he used to drive to a neighbouring house where he played cards. James went to the camp where an identity parade was held and he identified the two attackers. They were arrested and sent back to America.

There was a very big attendance at the funeral. The American army was represented by a Catholic padre. Edward was an Air Raid Warden and fellow wardens formed a guard of honour. On October 10 1942 the New

Clenaghans at Clenaghans: Fifteen different Clenaghan family cousins at a recent get together at Clenaghans Restaurant, Craigavon, following Michael Ferguson`s first communion. Michael lives in Vancouver and came over for the ceremony held earlier at St Joseph`s Church, Glenavy.

York Times reported that the two Americans were sentenced to ten years` hard labour and dishonourably discharged after being convicted at a court martial of voluntary manslaughter.

In the same year – 1942 - Britain was about half way through the Second World War and the Irish-Scottish cattle dealing business run by the three Clenaghan brothers was booming. Hugh had moved to Dublin out of the way of the troubles in Northern Ireland and James and John were living near Dumfries having moved to Scotland from Northern Ireland several years earlier.

James never went to school because education, it appears, was not insisted on in the Clenaghan household or possibly more likely the family needed the money that James was able to earn. Or possibly, James was needed for work in the family farm.Schooling was available but compulsory school attendance (for those aged between five and ten) was not made law until eleven years after he was born.

But although school beckoned and James could have been attending, he spent much of his boyhood helping in Lisburn livestock market according to his last living child, his daughter Sheila, now 100 and living in a retirement home in the south of England. At Lisburn market, he knew of a lot of rich men who were cattle dealers and while still a boy he decided that he too wanted to be a rich cattle dealer.

He earned coppers driving the cattle along the roads to and from the market and eventually was able to buy his first pig. He was not yet ten, according to Sheila.He continued to buy animals until, when he was 17 he rented a small farm and with his brothers John and Hugh started his life-long cattle dealing business. Cattle were bought in Ireland, fattened and sold in Scotland.

When he was 26 he decided to transfer all his operations to Scotland, to a farm in Ayrshire and later to the village of Terregles near Dumfries. John and Hugh stayed in Ireland and continued to run the business from there. That arrangement continued for about half a century. James had a relatively peaceful life with a family of 12 until his death at Terregles at the age of 91.

In comparison, his younger brother and business partner, Hugh had a life of struggle and personal heartbreak. The struggle centred mainly on the Irish nationalists` fight for home rule. That struggle, that had already forced James to leave Northern Ireland, eventually forced Hugh to do the same, except that he moved of Dublin in the Irish Republic where eventually he died at the age of 85.

 Hugh was born at Brackenhill, Lisburn on April 20 1875. When he was 25 he married Teresa Gillen daughter of Henry Gillen of the Packenhan Arms Hotel, Crumlin, about 12 miles away. Sadly, the marriage lasted only eight years. Teresa died in 1908 of meningitis. Hugh was joined at the funeral by his brothers John and James. Significantly, the brothers` cattle dealing interests attracted representatives of a steamship company and a railway company to the funeral.

Hugh remarried three years later, on July 29 1911. His bride was Mary O`Dwyer and the couple had three sons in quick successon. James Dominic was born on August 4 1913, son John Augustine was born on August 24 1914 and son, Hugh Cecil, born on February 7 1916.The family lived in Lisburn at Antrim Road and at Delta, North Circular Road. The house, Delta was sold in 1917. The reason for the sale, according to the advertising was that Hugh "had purchased a farm residence."

Shortly before that sale, the house, Delta, featured in a case at the town`s magistrates` court when several boys were charged with stealing property. Thefts from property may have been common in Lisburn at the time. But surely, never a theft of a whole property!

However, a solicitor at the court hearing following the theft told of such a theft. According to a local newspaper the solicitor had the whole court in stitches when he said he knew of a house in the town that had been "practically carried away by thieves- brick stone and iron".The solicitor added: "When the owner of the house was due to move in he found nothing but a piece of ground. He wanted to know where his house had gone." That incident may have got a court laughing. But other attacks, thefts, riots and arson attacks a few years later in Lisburn in August 1920 were very far from a laughing matter. One newspaper report spoke of a pogrom - an organized massacre of a particular ethnic group - in this case, Catholics.

The Clenaghans, of course, were Catholics.

CATHOLICS ARE MASSACRED

The report said that Catholic families in Bachelor`s Walk. Lisburn, had all their personal possessions - everything they owned- dragged from their homes and set on fire in the street. "Only the fact that Bachelor`s Walk formed a terrace saved them from being burned. The loyalist rioters realised there was a risk of the whole street being destroyed along with many Protestant- owned houses," said the report

The riots also brought great destruction to the Clenaghan family`s Lisburn property. The value of this property amounted to many hundreds of pounds and badly affected the brothers` cattle dealing business. And,

Wrecked after Swanzy riots- Hugh Clenaghan`s Lisburn home.

separate from this, a serious family falling out resulting in a court case five years later, must also have badly affected the business. The court case is described later in the story.

The 1920 Lisburn riots, remembered as the Swanzy riots, seem largely to have been forgotten. They followed the assassination in Lisburn of Royal Irish Constabulary District Inspector Oswald Ross Swanzy in front of worshippers leaving Lisburn Cathedral on a quiet sunny Sunday.

The assasination led to days of vicious looting and rioting, forcing many of the town's Catholics to flee. The events, a significant but not well known event in Lisburn's rich history, were part of the wider story of the War of Independence (1919-1922) on the island of Ireland. The riots were described in the newspaper, the Belfast Newsletter at the time,"like a scene from Dante`s Inferno."

The newspaper said this: "As darkness fell upon the scene, the flames of burning houses lit the sky, and the efforts of the local fire brigade had but little effect. In many instances the buildings were gutted before midnight, and in these places smouldering fires were seen with fitful tongues of flame bursting forth and running along the windows and walls; but in Bow Street several establishments were a seething mass of fire, while great clouds of red smoke hung overhead."

The report continued: "The full fury of the crowd found vent in the afternoon, shortly after the murder, and a number of persons said to have sympathy with Sinn Fein were injured. There was a great deal of looting, and reports were to be heard of bursting barrels of liquor burning licensed premises. Altogether, the scene was weird in the extreme as from a scene in Dante's Inferno."

Afterwards there was 300 compensation claims made by Lisburn residents and businesses. The total claimed was £840,595. Many claims were never made because the people affected had fled the city.Hugh Clenaghan claimed £14,500 for the destruction of his lovely newly built house, Russianurb, and its contents, together with outbuildings and two recently erected villas.(Based on established tables, I estimate that figure to be the equivalent of £780,000 today.)

In his claim Hugh said his business was exporting 10,000 head of store cattle every year.(Based on the 2022 Carlisle average price of £1,300 per head of the same cattle, I estimate that figure to be £13,000,000 today). The cattle sheds of his brother John were destroyed by fire and he was awarded £2,500 (£121,000 today). These facts and figures about the Swanzy riots are from a data base at the Irish Linen Centre and Lisburn Museum.

Hugh`s troubles continued after the riots and another son, Oliver was born on November 3 1921. He lived for only eight days. Seven years later, in 1928, there was another death in the family when John Augustine fell 200 feet while hunting birds` eggs on Ireland's Eye, a small uninhabited island off the coast of County Dublin at Howth, an outer suburb of Dublin. He was 14.Hugh and his family were then living in Dublin having moved there in the years following the Swanzy riots.

Four years after the death of John, another son, Desmond, died aged 14 but I have not been able to establish details of his death. Moving on to the year 1948, two events involving Hugh were recorded in the press. On April 16, he sold some building land together with accommodation named as Tonagh, Causeway End, Lisburn and in June there was the wedding of his third son, 22 year old Hugh Junior at University Church, Dublin.

The family`s address was given as Wynford House, Merrion Road, Ballsbridge, Dublin. Bridegroom Hugh`s bride was Margaret, third daughter of Mrs and the late Patrick Phelan of Aughrim, 44 miles away. Wynford House is now a hotel and is described on its web site as "A magnificent Edwardian accommodation situated in the prestigious embassy district of Ballsbridge, just 3 minutes from the city centre."

Hugh died in Dublin on February 8 1961, aged 85.His brother James died In Terregles 23 years later, in 1984. He was 91. Both were wealthy men.

POCKETS FULL OF GOLD COINS

Just how wealthy? Both had been successful cattle dealers in business together for many years. James as a young man, soon after arriving in Scotland, was reputed to to be "the most desirable bachelor in Scotland, his pockets full of gold coins," his daughter Sheila recalls.

She added: "When he drove his pony and trap through Annan, Dumfriesshire, on his way to Carlisle market I am told that my mother always put on her best clothes and went outside to wash the steps so that he would notice her. Clearly she succeeded and in 1907 they were married."

The girl James married was Annie Toner, who was 29, born at at Bath Street, Annan. Her mother owned a baker`s shop in the town. James was 39.The ceremony was at St Xavier Church, Waterside (Ayrshire) on October 14 1908.  James`s father was recorded at the wedding as John Clenaghan, a farmer, and his mother Bridget Clenaghan, formerly Flannagan. The bride`s father was recorded as Thomas Tonner, and her mother as Anne Divine.

A year after he was married, James purchased a big house, Nylestrom complete with stable and grounds in the Noblehill area of Dumfries. He gave the house an Irish name, Emerald Park, and lived there for three years. It was at Emerald Park that Stanella`s mother Anne was born on October 13 1910 followed by her brother James, born on October 16 1912. Emerald Park is now a hotel called The Old Town House.

From Emerald Park the family moved to the mansion, Terregles House, which they rented for twelve years until the house and its contents were sold by the Constable-Maxwell family in the early 1930s to James. It was there that James brought up his big family. James had eleven children, a twelfth, Hugh, died at a very young age. In order of birth these were: Nora, Mary, John, Anne, James, Bridget, Margaret, Patricia, Freddie, Dorothy and Sheila. John emigrated to Canada but sadly died eight years later, in a hotel fire in Rouyn-Noranda, Quebec.

Terregles House was one of a number of country houses in the area requisitioned for use by the Norwegian army during the Second World War. The Norwegians had escaped from their country in June 1940 after the German occupation and with their king and other Norwegian exiles had found refuge in the area around Dumfries.The king who was 67 had narrowly escaped being captured by the Germans .Two months later he reached Britain on the destroyer HMS Devonshire

GIFT OF A CHRISTMAS TREE.

While living in Terregles House and other places around Dumfries, the Norwegians planned commando and parachutist's raids on the Germans occupying their country. In one raid a party of Norwegians parachuted in and blew up an industrial facility used by the Germans to make "heavy water" which was intended for use in the development of a German atomic bomb.

On another raid, a 20 metre Christmas tree was brought back to Britain. It was admired so much that the Norwegian king decided to give it to Britain. It was erected in Trafalgar Square as a thank you from the Norwegians for British support.There was no electric lights then because there was still a blackout. But the tree was evergreen with defiant hope. When the war ended, the king returned to Norway. The Norwegian people remembered the gift and continued the tree giving tradition which has gone on to this day

The Norwegians who lived in Terregles House also did some remembering when the war ended. They put on a party in the village's Memorial Hall for all the Terregles villagers, as a way of saying thank you for the hospitality. By then some of the Norwegians had married local girls and planned to settle in the area. At the party, the Norwegians handed over a miniature ship in glass case as a gift to the village. Sadly, since then the ship has vanished.

What about the Clenaghan family during the war? They moved out from Terregles House to make room for the Norwegians and moved into a house called Learig in Castle Douglas Road, Dumfries. Annie, James's wife went into business and bought and sold furniture in the Dumfries area. It was about this time that James bought Palmerston Park, the home of Queen of the South football club and other Dumfries properties.

THE ESTATE IS BROKEN UP

Let us turn back to the First World War. There was other changes to Terregles House and the estate surrounding it, particularly in the years immediately afterwards. The estate was one of several similar estates throughout the country which were bought by the government in 1924 and divided into smallholdings for soldiers who had returned to civilian life.

The house was not included in the government purchase. As I said earlier, the house and its contents which had been owned by the powerful Maxwell family for several centuries were rented to James and sold to him in the early 1930s. His brothers Hugh and John continued to look after the Irish end of the business and transported most of the cattle through the Cumbria port of Workington or the Scottish port of Stranraer.

From these ports they were either driven by rail to the now- closed Maxwelton Station which is about two miles from Terregles, or driven along the road to Terregles. Each road journey would have been more than 70 miles which it is thought would have taken a week or more.

Today, driving cattle along a main road for 70 miles seems very improbable. Of course, 80 or more years ago there would have been very few motor vehicles on the roads. Some people who live in the village of Terregles and remember the Clenaghan family are certain that such cattle drives did take place.

CATTLE THIEVES AND CATTLE DISPUTES

And if there are doubts about "cattle drives" there are doubts too about how successful James Clenaghan was as a cattle dealer. Certainly he seems to have amassed considerable wealth and he gave much of that wealth away to Catholic institutions. But amassing considerable wealth from cattle dealing was not without its difficulties. One of these was cattle thieving.

One daring thief called at the Clenaghan's farm at Terregles after James had left the farm for the day. The thief said he had been asked by James to collect some cattle and drive them to Dumfries. He was given delivery of fifteen cattle which he drove to Dumfries along the main road and sold them at one of the town's cattle marts.

He was given a cheque for £180 (the equivalent of nearly £12,500 today). This he cashed at a Dumfries bank. Then he disappeared. Police were never able to trace him.

As I said earlier, the cattle dealing business

Before the blast! Terregles House as the Maxwells knew it.

in 1925 was claimed to be handling 10,000 cattle a year which I estimated to be £13,000,000 a year at today`s cattle prices.

But how much of this wealth was the result of the efforts of James Clenaghan and how much of it was the result of the efforts of his two brothers, Hugh and John? I pose the questions because the business, like all businesses, did not run smoothly all the time as the court case I mentioned previously proved.

The case, in 1925, revealed some of the story of how the Clenaghan wealth was created. The case was unusual because it involved all the three Clenaghan brothers and was a sequel to a serious disagreement between them.

It is not often that a disagreement between brothers ends in court. And it must be almost unheard of for brothers running the same business to fall out and then try to settle things in court.But that is what happened at Dumfries when James sued his brother Hugh following a disagreement over the business in which they both played leading parts.

In court the falling out became a ding dong battle of twists and turns. Both men were described as cattle dealers, James living at Terregles House and Hugh living at Ardeevin, North Circular Road, Dublin. A report of the case- in the Court of Session- filled several columns of the weekly newspaper, the Dumfries Standard. It is from that report that this account is based.

The court case seems to have been sparked off by a circular letter sent out by Hugh to farmer customers and to other cattle dealers. The letter said that future orders for cattle would be dealt with, not by James as was usual previously, but by Hugh. The implication was that Hugh now owned the business.

James was furious. He strongly objected to the letter so he started the court action which he said was aimed at stopping the letter and stopping any similar letters in future. James`s court action, he said, also aimed to stop Hugh marking his cattle with James`s marks or brands. James also sought compensation- a payment from Hugh of £2,000 (£135,000 at today`s prices).

James told the court that he had a large number of customers for Irish cattle, both in Scotland and England. Up to a short time previously he had employed Hugh as his agent in Ireland to buy the cattle. The arrangement between them was this: James paid Hugh the price paid for the cattle, plus the cost of transport plus a commission. James then sold the cattle direct to his customers in Scotland and England. Hugh had no direct dealings with the customers.

James told the court that a few weeks previously he had a dispute with Hugh. The upshot was that Hugh then wrote to him breaking off any business connection. However, said James, the position changed and the two of them came to another arangement allowing Hugh to sign cheques, including cheques to himself in payment for cattle he had bought, plus the cost of transport, and his commission.

This new arrangement did not last many days, said James, and Hugh told him this arrangement also was at an end. James said that he later discovered that Hugh had bought a large number of cattle in Ireland and sold them on to customers in Scotland and England who had ordered them. This said James was "A direct breach of faith."

James had also discovered that Hugh had issued the controvertial circular to Scottish and English customers saying that future orders for cattle would be dealt with by him and not by James. The persons who bought the cattle in Scotland were well known customers who had dealt for many years with the firm.

TRYING TO STEAL THE CATTLE BUSINESS

James said the circular maintained that Hugh was the owner of the cattle dealing business when in fact Hugh was only an agent in the business. The circular also claimed that the customers were Hugh`s customers when in fact they were the customers of James.James said that the circular also falsely claimed that he had been employed by Hugh but his services had since been dispensed with.

James said that purpose of the circular was nothing less than to steal his business and injure him in the eyes of the customers and the public. He said the £2,000 he sued for was "reasonable compensation" for the injury inflicted by Hugh.

Hugh then gave more evidence. And what he said was was in many respects quite different from James`s version. Hugh said that for many years he and James and the third brother, John, had been partners or "joint adventurers" in the business of buying cattle in Ireland and selling them in Scotland. He said he originally received one third of the profits but latterly he received a fixed sum per head of cattle as his share of the profits.

Hugh said there was later arrangement under which he had been allowed to draw cheques on James`s bank.This arrangement had been agreed because of James`s failure to to pay him sums due as his partner in the "joint adventure." Hugh said he later had to end the partnership because James had instructed another person, John McNally of Armagh, to buy cattle for him in Ireland.

Not only that, he had instructed Mr McNally to mark the purchased cattle with the mark that up to then had been used to denote cattle purchased by the brothers Clenaghan.Hugh agreed that for many years he had acted as agent to James in buying cattle in various parts of Ireland and was paid by James for the cattle plus expenses for transporting the cattle, plus a commission. But earlier in 1925 there was delay in his receiving payment so he wrote to James saying he intended to end the arrangement.

Hugh said he subsequently supplied cattle to Mr James Hamilton of Garlieston, Wigtownshire. He had paid for the cattle plus a profit of 10s. per head. Five shillings of that went to James and the other five shillings went half to himself (Hugh) and half to John. After the partnerhip ended there had been further orders from Mr Hamilton. Referring to the circular, Hugh said it had no great effect because it went to only four buyers. He denied that the circular was issued with the intention of appropriating James`s business or injuring him in any way.

Hugh then went on to describe how the business started. He recalled that the three brothers started the business in Ireland prior to 1898. They were then living with their father, a farmer in Lisburn who made over certain sums of money to each son and opened a bank account for the three under the name of Clenaghan Brothers.

Their cattle were mainly from the west of Ireland and were marked with a mark used only by the Clenaghan brothers. Profits were shared equally between the three brothers.

Hugh said that James was in the habit of travelling on the ship with the cattle to see to their sale in Scotland. Later in 1898, James withdrew from the business and was paid out his share of the capital and the profits. The business, said Hugh, was carried on by himself and John under the name of J. and H. Clenaghan. It continued to do well and about three years later, James re-joined the business, selling the cattle in Scotlnd and remitting the cash to the J. and H. Clenaghan account.

About the year 1909, James went to live in Dumfries and started in business as a farmer. To enable him to do this, he (Hugh) and John gave a £2,250 guarantee to the bank. The three brothers continued with the cattle dealing business and employed a Mr Samuel Clark as a canvasser. His cost was shared equally between the brothers.

The purchase of the farm allowed them to rest the cattle before they were sent to a buyer. As a charge for resting the cattle James was allowed to credit himself with the usual auctioneer`s charges. However in or about 1921, James complained that he was not being paid enough for resting the cattle. It was then agreed between the three brothers that instead of sharing the profits, the brothers in Ireland should receive a fixed profit of five shillings for each animal shipped.

They would advise James of the cost of buying the cattle in Ireland and embarking them on board a steamer. As soon as the cattle were sold he should remit that amount plus their profit of 5s per head. James was to pay the expenses of the cattle`s transit and their keep in Scotland and retain, as his profit, any balance which there might be once the cattle were sold. The arrangement continued until 1923 when John retired from the business.

Two years later Hugh said he complained to James of delay in submitting the price of the cattle and the profits. But after a new negotiation, the business arrangement was allowed to continue.

However, shortly afterwards he discovered that James had breached the agreement by giving orders to another man, Mr John McNally of Armagh to buy cattle for him and ship them with the Clenaghan Brothers` mark. He therefore told James that the partnership was at an end. The Dumfries Standard does not give the outcome of the case except to say the case was remitted to a Procedure Roll. This is the name given to a court hearing on a legal issue.

NIFTY MANOEUVRES OVER £1M HOUSE SALE

A year after that court case, James was again heavily involved with Terregles House and its possible sale to the government. According to his family there was some nifty manoeuvring. James had heard in advance about this possible sale so on the day before, he went to Edinburgh where the sale was being handled and offered £5 more than the government had bid.

He got the house for £12,005 which today is the equivalent to over £1 million. His £5 is the equivalent of about £330 today. To recoup some, if not all of the cash he had laid out, he allowed a company to establish a sawmill on the land and got the firm to cut down most of the trees on the estate. From the sale of this timber he recovered his £12,005 and more, according to the family.

The sawmill was not the only business on the estate. There was also a pig factory in which James had had a twenty per cent share in the company that ran it. The meat was sold through the various butchers in neighbouring Dumfries who also had shares in the Terregles company.

Today, the Clenaghans are remembered in the Terregles area as a friendly family always ready to make the big house and its grounds available to the village for garden fetes and other village events. The family mixed very little socially with village people and were treated as just a bit above the average villager and as a result, they were kept somewhat at a distance.

Local people wishing to be critical of the Clenaghans would point to the family`s comparative short stay of about 30 years in the village compared to the many generations of Maxwells who previously occupied the

big house for centuries. The critics`conclusion was that the Clenaghans "exploited" the estate and "took" from it much of what the very creative Maxwells had built up over the centuries.

GIFTS TO A CATHOLIC SCHOOL

The same accusation cannot be said of a Dumfries Catholic school, St.Joseph`s College (left), which James Clenaghan did much to support in its early years. His gifts are remembered in a plaque in the porch of the school church.

Arguably, James Clenaghan was the school`s biggest donor. The college lost a good friend and a great benefactor with his death" said the school in a tribute. His activity and business acumen earned for him a rising importance in the cattle trade and prosperity followed as a matter of course.

"He was ever ready to lend assistance to charitable causes and in this he was ably seconded by Mrs. Clenaghan. When special efforts were being made to raise funds for the erection of our memorial church, he was a most generous contributor providing most of the prizes for the draw which raised a magnificent sum in 1919," said the school tribute.

"It was through him also that the school was able to acquire Barkerfield, now known as Maryfield for their college playing fields. It is however in connection with church that Mr. and Mrs. Clenaghan are best remembered, their financial contributions and active assistance helping greatly towards it erection," said the tribute.

St. Joseph's College was founded as a boarding school for boys in 1875, by the Marist Brothers, a Roman Catholic teaching order, which originated in France. The school opened with twelve pupils. The college was originally housed in what had been the Dumfries Infirmary, opened in 1878. It was purchased on behalf of the Marist Brothers in 1874 by a Mr. Murphy of Dumfries after the Infirmary moved to new quarters.

The college was to be used for the training of young men for the Marist Brotherhood, and owing to the demand for boarding school education the school accepted the first boarders soon after it opened. The accomodation was soon found to be too small so in 1877 the Brothers purchased the property known as Laurel Mount, on the Craigs Road, and built a new training school for the young brothers and renamed it Mount St. Michael.

St. Joseph`s College continued in the old Infirmary until further need for expansion caused the Brothers to build the present main building in 1909. The college church was started in 1919. In 1971, the Marist Brothers and the Dumfries Education Authority made an arrangement whereby all Roman Catholic boys of secondary school age living in Dumfrieshire, could attend the college, and by 1975, the centenary year, the college roll had risen to almost 600.

In 1981, the college was taken over formally by Dumfries and Galloway Regional Council to become one of the four co-educational schools within the borough of Dumfires.

MARY QUEEN OF SCOTS

There were at least two earlier Terregles Houses, both sometimes referred to as castles. They were built for defensive purposes as well as homes of the Maxwells. The first was a wooden structure and the second built of stone. Both have long since disappeared. One of the two houses, or castles, was visited on at least two occasions by Mary Queen of Scots, perhaps the most famous figure in Scotland`s royal history.

The first was in 1563 when she spent the night there with her privy council, apparently to arrange a peace treaty with England but really to win support of Sir John Maxwell, head of the Maxwell dynasty. Mary`s second visit was five years later when she was fleeing south after her defeat at Langside, near Glasgow by the forces of the Earl of Moray. Maxwell escorted her to safety at Terregles House.

She stayed for some days while she consulted with her advisers whether she should return to France or throw herself on the mercy of her cousin, Queen Elizabeth. Against the advice of Maxwell, she decided on the latter course and sailed across the Solway in a fishing boat making her way to England where instead of getting help she was imprisoned by Elizabeth and beheaded at the age of 44.

The last remaining Terregles House was a late 18th-century red sandstone country mansion built in 1789, the year of the French revolution when the aristocracy in that country was being stripped of its privileges. Quite the contrary situation in Scotland as far as the Maxwell aristocracy was concerned. The magnificent Terregles House represented a new peak in the Maxwell power and wealth.

It was recognised as an outstanding example of a Scots` nobleman`s house. The stone was quarried at Dalbeattie, fifteen miles away.The house contained more than 120 rooms including a pheasantry, a beer cellar, billiard room, gun room and games room. It had as many windows as days in the year. There were two halls, a dining room with a dog grate, 14 bedrooms for residents and four servants` rooms, a private laundry, morning and drawing rooms, private chapel and a library.

Terregles House and the two earlier houses or castles had each in turn served as the seat of the Lords Herries of Terregles, and later the Earls of Nithsdale, until William Maxwell, the 5th Earl, forfeited his titles in 1716 following a Jacobite uprising the previous year.

RESCUE FROM THE TOWER OF LONDON

Lady Winifred Maxwell, the granddaughter of the 5th Earl, served as heir general to to her father, inheriting the Terregles property. Lady Winifred achieved fame through two notable rescues. In 1716 she rescued her husband the earl, from the Tower of London where he was imprisoned. The rescue took place on the day before the earl`s planned execution.

Thirty one years later, in 1746 she rescued Bonnie Prince Charlie after the Battle of Culloden. The prince was in a desperate situation on the isle of South Uist and needed to escape from the English Butcher, the Duke of Cumberland.

The Tower of London rescue is as thrilling as any current TV or film thriller and follows the Jacobite rising of 1715. The Earl took part in the rising but was captured by Government troops at Preston along with six other peers and taken to London.The seven prisoners were trussed up like chickens and led through the city on horseback past jeering crowds. Finally they were locked up in the tower.

Fortunately, since his capture, the Earl had managed to get a letter to his wife, the countess who was in Terregles. She immediately made plans to go to London. But knowing that the house might be seized by the Provost of Dumfries, she and a gardener buried writs and private papers in the grounds in the middle of the night. She dismissed all the staff and though she was pregnant and expecting a child soon, she set off for London.

She rode to Newcastle. But the seats on the London coach which she planned to join were all booked. So she rode on to York where she managed to get a seat on the coach and arrived in London exhausted and racked with fever. The earl was brought to trial in Westminster Hall on January 19, 1716 along with the six other peers. He pleaded guilty to high treason and ordered to be sentenced to death on February 19.

When the countess arrived at the tower she managed to bribe the guards to allow her visits to see her husband. During those visits, she carefully studied the guard's movements. The countess then petitioned King George for a pardon but was unsuccessful. So she devised a daring and ingenious plan to get her husband free. He had only two days to live.

First, she returned to the tower where she won over the guards by pretending her petition had been granted by the king. To celebrate her joy at this, she pressed a few coins into their hands. The next day, on the eve of the execution date, she returned to the tower with two friends, a Mrs Mills and Mrs Morgan, and managed to get permission to see the earl, one person at a time.

First visitor was Mrs. Morgan who was wearing an extra cloak and petticoat. These she took off and left in the room. Mrs Mills then went in, sobbing loudly with her face covered with a handkechief. She put on the clothes left by Mrs Morgan, leaving her own clothes and continued with a big show of tears and other distress. The countess put her arm around her and urged her to be brave and calm.

When the countess went in, she brushed white paint on her husband`s black eyebrows and rubbed rouge on his cheeks. She told him to dress in the clothes Mrs Mills had discarded.

She then held the earl firmly by the arm as he buried his face in Mrs Mill's handkerchief she walked between him and the guards pretending to be in state of great agitation and then led him past the guards. They had become confused by all the comings and goings and by diversions created by the countess.

As the earl was led away to safety by Mrs Mills and Mrs Morgan, the countess returned to his room where she carried on an imaginary conversation with him. In the cell she could be overheard taking a solemn and affectionate leave of the earl and promising to return to see him in the morning when she hoped she would have some good news for him. As she left the cell she locked the door so that it could only be opened from the inside. She told the guards that the earl was saying his prayers and did not want candles brought until he sent for them.

It is recorded that the escape of the earl created a deep sensation at the Court in London and throughout the kingdom. The earl was hidden in different places in London for some time until he was disguised in a livery coat and taken first to Dover, and then to Calais, and eventually to the exiled Jacobean court in Rome where he died in 1744.

Immeditely after the earl`s escape, the countess returned to Terregles to retrieve the family writs which she had buried. She found them perfectly safe and dry. She immediately sent them to relatives at Traquair House, in Peeblesshire. She joined her husband in Rome and survived him by five years, dying there in 1749.

Another Lady Winifred, granddaughter of the countess, returned to Scotland to try to build up the old castle at Terregles and the estates, now far removed from their former glory.

Lady Winifred Maxwell

ROBBIE BURNS` WELCOME HOME.

The poet Robert Burns (1759-1796) wrote the following poem"Niths-dale`s Welcome Home" to commemorate the occasion. He was living at Dumfries at the time and frequently visited Terregles:

"The noble Maxwells and their powers

Are coming o`er the Border,

And they`ll gae big Terreagles Towers

And set them a in order.

And they declare Terreagles fair

For their abode they chuse it.

There` no a heart in a the land

But`s lighter at the news o`t."

Lady Winifred apparently gave up on building the old castle and 1789 she and and her husband, William Haggerston Constable of Everingham, commissioned the Yorkshire architect Thomas Atkinson to build the new house. It became home to the Constable-Maxwell family and their seven children. Sir Robert Smirke was employed to extend the house and build a new stable block in 1831.

In 1848 Lady Winifred's grandson, William Constable-Maxwell, obtained an Act of Parliament restoring him as the descendant of William Maxwell, 5th Earl of Nithsdale, and ten years later the House of Lords declared him the 10th Lord Herries of Terregles. In 1875 Henry Constable-Maxwell of Terregles, another grandson of Winifred Maxwell and brother of the 10th Lord Herries, inherited Traquair House from a cousin. The house is claimed to be the oldest continually occupied house in Scotland.

In the same year Henry's nephew, Marmaduke Francis Constable-Maxwell, the 11th Lord Herries, married Angela Fitzalan-Howard, a grand-daughter of the 13th Duke of Norfolk. According to some historians it may be that the Constable-Maxwells' focus shifted from Terregles with the introduction of new property to the family. Other people maintain that the Maxwells left Terregles because they had run out of money.

In 1924, the government bought the estate, but not the house, and divided the land into smallholdings for soldiers who had returned from the First World War. The house and its contents were sold by the Constable-Maxwell family to James Clenaghan. After the Second World War the majority of the house was boarded up and unused.

Some time after 1955 the Clenaghans moved into the lodge at Terregles House, which had been built in the 1880's about 100 years after the main house. The main house lay empty and was suffering badly from dry rot. The furniture from the main house was sold off at auction after Mary, James Clenaghan's daughter, had selected what she wanted for the lodge. She lived there for a few years then moved to Dumfries. She died in Edinburgh in 1974.

Mary chose John Vardy, an architect living a short distance away in Terregles, to design the extensions. Mr Vardy`s daughter Erica told me that she had in her garden two decorative sandstone balls from the garden of Terregles House. Erica remembers the Clenaghans when they lived at the Lodge. One member of the family she recalls particularly was Dorothy, the second youngest, who had mental health problems.

The treatment she got for these was barbaric. It involved removing part of her brain in a procedure known as a lobotomy. This invoved the use of an ice axe. Is there any wonder that the lobotomy is now generally considered one of the most barbaric treatments in the history of modern medicine?

Probably the most notable person to have undergone the treatment is Rosemary Kennedy, sister of U.S. President John F. Kennedy. Like Dorothy Clenaghan, she was in her twenties. As a child and young adult, Kennedy had mild developmental delays that impaired her performance in school. As Rosemary got older, she reportedly began to experience violent seizures and temper tantrums, lashing out at those around her.

Seeking a treatment to ease her outbursts and fearing that Rosemary's behavior would create a bad reputation for herself and for the whole family, Rosemary's father arranged a lobotomy for Rosemary when she was 23 years old. Throughout the entire procedure, Rosemary is said to have been awake, speaking with doctors, and reciting poems to nurses. Doctors knew the procedure was over when she stopped speaking.

Following the procedure she became severely disabled. She was unable to function independently, and was institutionalized for the remainder of her life. It is not known whether Dorothy suffered a similar fate as a result of her lobotomy.

In 1957 Terregles House was sold to Mr William Hodge, a seed merchant and farmer of Terreglestown and it was unoccupied for some time. It was demolished with explosives by the army in 1962, because it had become infested with dry rot.

`A PRECISION JOB BY SAPPERS`

That demolition was a sensation locally and much further afield.... "A precision job by sappers" is how the local paper, the Dumfries Standard reported it. The newspaper went on: "A monument of 175 years of Scottish history disappeared in a split second. The army pressed a button, there was a deafening bang and Terregles House, Dumfries, built in the year of the French Revolution became a mound of dusty rubble.

"The mansion was a relic of an era when Scottish noblemen whiled away their leisure time shooting in the morning, wining in the afternoon, and dining in the evening".

A party of Scottish sappers, all Royal Engineers` territorials, led by Major Dick Hough spent five days preparing for the big bang. They placed 316 pounds of plastic explosives at strategic points in the building. Then, local people, photographers and and the Press were invited to watch as Piper John Fairhurst played a lament and finally the button for demolition was pressed by Warrant Officer James White. Unfortunately, nothing happened and the operation was adjourned to the next day when the demolition finally took place.

What remains of Terregles House nearly sixty years after that explosion?

The site has the remnants of a country estate landscape where the house, the Italianate terraced gardens, a flower garden and water features have now been lost. The former stables, a category A listed building, have been converted into housing. The land is now under grazing but the layout of the Italianate garden, and adjacent ladies walk and grotto are still discernible.

Extensive walls surround the property, which are thought to have been built by French prisoners of war in the 18th century. The wall is now broken in places, as parts of the estate have been sold off.

I set off to find out what remains of Terregles House one sunny day in June and made my way to the 40 acre Sunnyhill Farm, which has been formed from part of the extensive Italian gardens after being purchased from Mr Hodge in 1959. The farmhouse was built in 1964. It is on the site of a former temporary house which housed one of the estimated 20 gardeners which were employed by the Maxwells when the big house was in its heyday.

Terregeles Lodge built about a century ago now the home of David and Joan Wood who are pictured here.

Near the farmhouse are the sites of three more former gardeners` houses and site of a former stone house which was the home of the head gardener. Farmer Richard Crawshaw and his sister Valerie have a a herd of 30 Galloway cattle. The couple came to the farm with their parents who had a Welsh shepherding background as well as a hardware retail business background in Dumfries.

Their main farm building is a 100 foot long single storey sandstone structure, built in 1789, at the same time as the big house and was originally used daily by the big house team of gardeners for such jobs as potting.The structure has a cellar, originally used for storing vegetables. Thick sandstone slabs on the cellar floor help to keep the temperature low. The Crawshaws have the structure divided in to five units which are used for storage and for housing cattle.

Garden shed: Richard and Valerie Crawshaw at their Sunnyhill Farm in the gardens of Terregles House. Maxwell gardeners worked in the building, right, which is now housing cattle.

A series of greenhouses were once connected with the structure together with the associated boiler houses supplying the heat. Tropical fruit and vegetables were grown including an orangery, a dedicated building where orange and other fruit trees were protected during the winter. Little of the greenhouses remain but much of the extensive series of pipes is still in place. Also still in place is an impressive fountain, once a focal point of the gardens and four statues. Several other statues have been destroyed.

Intact is an ice house (also known as ice well, ice pit or ice mounds). It is a building for storing ice throughout the year. Ice houses date from before electricity and the modern refrigerator. Ice houses are usually located partly or completely underground and are often built near the natural sources of ice in winter, such as rivers and freshwater lakes. During the winter, ice and snow would be taken into the ice house and insulated against melting with straw or sawdust. It would stay frozen for many months, even until the following winter.

During the Second World War, the Terregles ice house acted as as air raid shelter for the Norwegian soldiers who were billeted in the big house. The soldiers left their signatures on the walls of the ice house and are still there to see.

Getting near the remains of Terregles House is far from easy. The remains comprise a pile of stone hidden

Last relic of Terregles House - the Maxwell coat of arms now hanging in Maxwell Memorial Hall, Terregles.

from view by a thicket of bramble, weeds, grass and young trees. But from the gardens it is possible to see the site of the house and what remains of the very busy and productive estate that the enterprising Maxwell family built up before it was all abandoned in the last years of the 1800's.

It is thought that as many as 200 people were employed in the house and outside, manning enterprises, mentioned earlier, that included a saw mill, a butcher's premises, many boilers, water catchments for hydro electricity as well as the gardens. All that remains of Terregles House apart from the ruins, is the Maxwell coat of arms which adorned the staircase wall. It was hung in the Terregles village Maxwell Memorial Hall where it is still a feature.

In 1924, the Government bought the estate, but not the house, and divided the land into smallholdings for soldiers who had returned from the First World War. The house and its contents were sold by the Constable-Maxwell family to James Clenaghan. After the Second World War the majority of the house was boarded up and unused.

Some time after 1955 the Clenaghans moved into the lodge of Terregles House. It was built in the 1880's, about 100 years after the main house. The main house lay empty and, suffering badly from dry rot was blown up in 1964.

The explosion that destroyed Terregles House was a big event locally and nationally. Pictures appeared in the national press which Stanella saw and was greatly curious about. She was then 30 years old and living in Carlisle. The pictures set her off on a quest to find her roots. It was to be a tragically disappointing and fruitless quest lasting nearly half a century.

In that half century, Stanella discovered she was conceived and born in secrecy; she was denied a mother's love by the woman who gave birth to her; she was given away as a baby; she was denied the truth of her birth by the family that brought her up; she was denied that truth by her first husband; and on the verge of finally finding out that truth, again had it snatched from her, this time by the death of the woman who gave birth to her.

In today's apparently more enlightened times there would have been no "secrecy" because Stanella, as soon as she she could understand, would no doubt have been told the truth of her birth. Stanella would have been the last person to complain that she had "missed out," as all these chapters of denial played themselves out.

She would not have complained because she was always fiercely loyal to Jimmy and Bessie Henderson who brought her up and gave her a name and total security in a home she loved.

What about Stanella's mother, Anne? She had no part to play in her daughter's life. Did Anne miss out? As she got to old age and the path to her death, did Anne ever regret having given away Stanella? We shall never know. What we do know is that ten years or so, after giving Stanella away, Anne appears to have gained a secure marriage with three children.

But a happy life?

Life for Anne appears not to have been a continuous stream of happiness. According to her sister Margaret, every year on November 29 Anne cried to herself.That date was Stanella's birthday. Those birthday tears must surely have been tears of regret and tears of sadness about what might have been if only she had kept her baby.

Yes, Stanella might have replied...if only she had kept her baby.

ALZHEIMERS FOR SIX YEARS

When Stanella was 81 she was diagnosed with Alzheimers which caused her much pain and distress. There was no cure, just a gradual and cruel decline over six years.

At the very end of her life, she had problems with her breathing. On Friday October 9 2020, Stanella stopped eating and drinking and was sleeping all the time. On the following day she drifted into becoming unconscious. I rang for a doctor. Three paramedics arrived and examined her. They decided that as they could do nothing to help her she had to go into the Cumberland Infirmary, Carlisle. They started to get her ready.

I refused to allow her to go because the family wanted to keep her at home and because we knew that once she was inside the infirmary and its Covid restrictions, none of the family would have been allowed to see her.

Later the same day, Elaine noticed that Stanella's hands had started to go blue. At about 9 pm Dr. Patrick Gray arrived and after examining her he said there was nothing more he could do. This was no surprise. But what did cause a surprise to me was a comment by Dr Gray. Without prompting, he began to praise my care of Stanella over the six years since she started to become ill.

I felt embarrassed and I wondered if he dished out praise in this way to all the families of his patients. What he said was this: "If I had been in a similar situation to that of your wife, I would want you to look after me." I felt honoured and thanked him. I said that all members of our family had played equally important parts in caring for Stanella for six years.

Stanella died at 1.20 a.m. the following day, Monday, October 12. Most of the family - Elaine, Bryan, Keith,

Last supper - Stanella and her family in the shadow of her final illness. Left to right, Bryan, Jonathan, Elaine John and Keith.

Jonathan, Andy and myself were all there when she passed away. Afterwards, we chatted quietly together for about an hour.

Stanella`s body was taken away by Hudsons the undertakers at 11 am on the following day and the funeral was arranged for the 19th at Carlisle Crematorium.

FUNERAL AND A FINAL HOME COMING

On Friday (16th) Stanella`s body was brought back to Longlands Road for an hour. Then it was sealed down again for the funeral. This was conducted by the Upperby Catholic priest, Father Luiz Ruscillo. Stanella had been born and brought up as a Catholic but had not attended that church for some time. But she had attended other churches.

We felt she would have wished to be buried a Catholic. Father Luiz impressed us all with his great warmth and dignity. No singing was allowed in the service because of Covid restrictions and only 25 people were allowed to attend. The same number was the maximum allowed at the meal following the service.

We decided to buy one of the last remaining burial plots at Upperby Cemetery as a final home for Stanella`s ashes and also the final home of the ashes of our daughter, Alyson. Both deaths are also recorded in the crematorium`s Book of Remembrance.

The burial plot is not much more than a stone`s throw away from Ridgemount Road where Stanella spent her happiest days. For Stanella, number 11 remained for ever her home. It was the home that almost to her dying day she fought vainly to return to. It was fitting that she was buried so close to that home.

Elaine wrote the eulogy. Here is a section:

"Stanella`s family meant a lot to her and she spent her life running the home and bringing up her children, who all loved her greatly and have since given her much pride, pleasure and joy in the form of seven grandchildren and eight great grandchildren.

"To the grandchildren, Stanella was the classy and glamorous Nana, always available for homemade chips, girly chats and treats.

"And she also had much good advice such as: `Choose a classy perfume, make it yours and stick with it and the smell of Channel No 5.

"Stanella had a quiet, personal faith in God. She said her prayers every night and could still recite parts of the Latin Mass which she had been taught as a child.

"And so, today, we give thanks for Stanella,

For all that she was by nature and by grace,

For all that she was enabled to be and to do,

For all that made her so very special."

Stanella`s grave in Upperby Cemetery Carlisle.